Functional Behavioral Assessment and Intervention in Schools

A Practitioner's Guide–Grades 1-8

James L. McDougal
Sandra M. Chafouleas
Betsy Waterman

Research Press
2612 North Mattis Avenue
Champaign, Illinois 61822
[800] 519-2707
www.researchpress.com

Figure 2.1, "Carroll's Model of School Learning," reprinted from J.B. Carroll, 1963, *Teacher's College Record, 64,* p. 730.

Figure 2.2, "Analyzing Academic Problems: The Instructional Hierarchy," adapted from E.J. Daly, J.C. Witt, B.K. Martens, and E.J. Dool (1997), *School Psychology Review, 26,* pp. 554–574.

Copies of this book may be ordered from Research Press at the address given on the title page.

Composition by Publication Services, Inc.
Cover design by Linda Brown, Positive I.D. Graphic Design, Inc.
Printed by Malloy, Inc.

ISBN-13: 978–0–87822–555-2
ISBN-10: 0–87822–555-2
Library of Congress Control Number 2005936300

Contents

Figures and Tables

Figures

Tables

Worksheets

Acknowledgments

I would like to acknowledge my wife, Lisa, and my children, Ben and Cara, for the strength, security, structure, and humility I derive from them. In addition, I would like to acknowledge my mother, Roberta, for the energy, tenacity, and drive that she offers. Last, I would like to acknowledge my father, Thomas Robert, who will always be at the core of my intellectual curiosity and whose untimely departure left me with an increased appreciation for and deeper understanding of the journey on which we have embarked.

—J. L. M.

I would like to express my sincere thanks to family, friends, and colleagues for their support through this project.

—S. M. C.

I want to thank my husband, David Sargent, and my children for their support and patience in the long and sometimes frustrating process of bringing this book to fruition. I also want to thank Jim and Sandy for their thoughtful comments and collegial style, which made this process one that was beneficial for me in many ways and that goes well beyond simply the generation of this book.

—B. W.

CHAPTER 1

Introduction

Joey is a six-year-old attending first grade. Joey's mother abandoned him at the age of four, and his history suggests physical abuse on her part. He currently lives with his aunt. Joey's teacher has expressed concern about his disruptive classroom behavior. She states that the behavior occurs several times a week, usually after she gives directions either to Joey individually or to the whole class. At first, Joey ignores her verbal request; she then provides a physical prompt (a touch on his shoulder). When she does so, Joey's disruptive behavior erupts, continues until he is exhausted, and eventually ends in compliance. Joey's problem behaviors during these tantrums include spitting, throwing things, biting, and screaming. This pattern occurs despite the teacher's attempts to speak with Joey and have him use deep breathing and counting backward to calm himself when he is upset.

This case example describes a situation in which *functional behavioral assessment* (FBA) is helpful in accommodating a student with challenging behavior. In this case, the assessment might include looking at the types of teacher requests that precipitate Joey's tantrums, assessing the activities or academic task demands present when he tantrums, identifying alternatives to physical prompts for gaining his compliance, and possibly looking at nonschool factors—such as his history, home life, and community life—that may also influence his behavior in school. The FBA and intervention with Joey would seek to identify and modify those variables that predict and support his challenging behavior, while also teaching or helping him to use more adaptive behavior to meet his needs.

The focus of the FBA process is on identifying important conditions in the environment that influence a student's behavior and altering those conditions through the development and implementation of a *behavior intervention plan*, or BIP. Contemporary approaches to school-based FBA seek to identify changeable conditions in the classroom to reduce problematic student behavior. In addition, variables that are not easily changed—those within the child or outside the classroom—are also identified, and whenever possible, accommodations for these predictive conditions are also developed.

This volume offers school-based practitioners—including school psychologists, counselors, administrators, social workers, and teachers—a comprehensive resource for conducting feasible and effective functional behavioral assessment and creating appropriate behavior intervention plans. This book outlines the stages in the FBA process and, using case examples to illustrate the process, helps guide decisions about the use of the FBA for a variety of problems—from academic to behavioral, mild to severe. It also offers ideas for interventions that match a variety of common school-based problems and includes numerous user-friendly, repro-ducible worksheets. Practitioners should find the materials in this volume helpful in accommodating a wide range of students with challenging behavior in their classroom settings.

Functional Behavioral Assessment: Definition and Background

Functional behavioral assessment is a process for determining how a student's behavior is influenced and supported by conditions in the environment. FBA methods vary widely, from fairly simple descriptive techniques that rely on teacher and parent interviews to more time-consuming and complex techniques, employing direct observation and the testing of functional theories via manipulations of the environment.

The History of FBA

Early research on functional assessments primarily involved individuals possessing significant handicapping conditions, corresponding communicative delays, and severe behavioral problems, often related to self-injurious behavior. Researchers such as Carr (1977) and Iwata, Dorsey, Slifer, Bauman, and Richman (1982) exper-imentally investigated the "messages" children were sending by engaging in such behavior. They found that, although the behaviors looked similar, the reasons these children engaged in the behaviors were different. By systematically manipulating the environment, especially the consequences of the behaviors—in other words, what happened in response to them—these researchers were able to show, for instance, that although two children might engage in similar self-injurious behav-iors, one used it to elicit attention, whereas the other used it to escape a task or demand. Interventions matched to the *function* of the child's behavior were found to be more successful than those that were not functionally relevant. (For a review of this research, see Repp, 1994.)

FBA in Schools

From this tightly controlled and experimental process, functional behavioral assessment continued to evolve to include more informal and indirect methods (e.g., interviewing techniques), becoming feasible for applied use with more diverse populations (McDougal, Nastasi, & Chafouleas, 2005). With this expansion, researchers began applying this knowledge to behaviors evidenced in school settings. In addition to behavioral consequences, they found that other variables—such as task difficulty (Weeks & Gaylord-Ross, 1981), choice of task (Dyer, Dunlap, & Winterling, 1990), and instructional pace (West & Sloane, 1986)—had an effect on student behavior. In fact, a review of available literature on the use of FBA with high-incidence behaviors in schools has suggested that curriculum variables often have a functional relationship to problem behavior (Reid & Nelson, 2002). This finding is promising because these variables are under teacher control and thus modifiable.

Although the use of functional behavioral assessments has expanded considerably over the past few years, this approach continues to be viewed by many as useful primarily with children whose behavioral problems are severe. It is the premise of this book, however, that functional assessment may be used in a more proactive and preventative manner in a wide variety of situations and across a broad range of problems. The 2004 amendments to the Individuals with Disabilities Education Improvement Act (IDEA 2004; P. L. 108-446) mandate that special educators, psychologists, and other members of the individual education program (IEP) team use FBA and positive behavioral interventions when disciplining students with disabilities. Indeed, when used as an accommodation for behaviorally challenging students, FBA is consistent with the components of the No Child Left Behind (NCLB) legislation, which requires heightened emphasis on school accountability, increased focus on creating safe schools, and the provision of additional supports for children from disadvantaged settings.

The FBA process may be appropriate for use with children who demonstrate mild or moderate behavioral, academic, or communication problems. In addition, the process may be relevant in the following circumstances:

1. When designing effective prereferral interventions (prior to considering eligibility for special education)

2. When determining least restrictive environments for students receiving special education services

3. When developing accommodation plans or other positive behavioral supports for individual students, including IEPs and Section 504 plans

In fact, the FBA process may be one way to intervene before a problem escalates to the point that more restrictive and costly interventions are required.

Reasons for Conducting a Functional Behavioral Assessment

Although there are many good reasons for employing FBA and BIP procedures in the schools, we discuss briefly here some of the practical, legal, and ethical reasons for doing so.

Practical Reasons

Functional assessment is one way for school personnel to use limited resources to make effective and efficient decisions about how and when a student's problem behavior can be changed (e.g., McDougal, 1998). Intervention decisions made through a functional problem-solving process are more efficient than those made through an often lengthy trial-and-error approach. This practical reason for conducting FBA has been referred to as *conceptual relevance* (Erchul & Martens, 2002). Although more time initially may be spent selecting an intervention, making a correct decision can be more time efficient than quickly making a decision that fails and then must be reviewed again.

Although good school-based interventions can be as simple as posting class rules or rearranging classroom furniture, selecting the correct intervention for a given situation may be harder than it seems. In fact, in one survey of teachers, conducted by Lambert (1976), a high proportion of common classroom management strategies were found to be ineffective. A primary reason for this ineffectiveness was that treatment selection was arbitrary and made without consideration of "fit" with the situation—in other words, without consideration of the function of the behavior or feasibility of the intervention for use in the classroom. For example, a teacher might choose to use planned ignoring for a student who seeks attention by being verbally disruptive during class time. However, if the student's peers give their attention in the form of laughter, planned ignoring will be ineffective. Or a teacher might send a student to time-out for disrupting instruction. Yet, if the instruction is boring to the student, then time-out is likely to be an ineffective intervention because it allows him to escape the boring activity while doing nothing to enhance the activity's relevance for him. In both cases, the FBA process could have provided a method for identifying the reasons the child engages in the particular behavior so the teacher can employ an intervention that directly addresses the conditions influencing the behavior (see McDougal & Chafouleas, 2001).

Legal Reasons

Legal reasons also exist for engaging in a functional behavioral assessment and behavioral intervention planning. Similar to the 1997 amendments to the Individuals with Disabilities Education Act (IDEA; P. L. 105-17), the 2004 amendments require that FBA and BIP procedures be implemented when disciplining students with disabilities. Specifically, the legislation requires that regardless of disability, children removed from educational programming or placements for disciplinary reasons receive appropriate functional behavioral assessment and behavioral intervention services to ensure that the behavioral violation does not reoccur.

Beyond student discipline, based on the language in the last two revisions of IDEA, it is clear that lawmakers have intended greater emphasis on positive approaches to dealing with student behavior, as opposed to traditional exclusionary or punishment-based procedures. For example, it is now required that positive behavioral interventions and supports be considered in the IEP plan whenever the child's behavior impedes the child's learning or the learning of others. As summarized by Drasgow and Yell (2001), FBA should be considered if the problem behavior interferes with learning or presents a danger to the student or others, or when suspension to interim alternative placement is involved.

Ethical Reasons

The management of severe problem behaviors in the classroom is a growing challenge for teachers (see Biglan, 1995; Kauffman, 1997; Sprague, Sugai, & Walker, 1998; and Walker, Colvin, & Ramsey, 1995). Sugai, Sprague, Horner, and Walker (2000) estimated that, although students presenting severe behavioral problems in the schools represent only 1 to 5 percent of a school's population, these problems result in more than 50 percent of the incidents reported in school and consume large amounts of educators' and administrators' time and energy. Unfortunately, teachers often have limited resources to deal with this behavior, little training in effective behavioral management, and restricted access to administrative support (Horner, Diemer, & Brazeau, 1992). Typical school-based interventions, such as in-school or out-of-school suspension, are short-term solutions that do little to reduce ongoing problem behaviors or teach students new, more effective behavioral responses (Crone & Horner, 2000).

At best, severe problem behaviors divert teachers' energy away from instruction; at worst, they diminish the safety of schools. Thus FBA should be an integral part of the assessment of and intervention for disruptive behavior, not an isolated practice. An FBA conducted during the early stage of a problem can prevent escalation of that problem, avoiding more costly interventions such as expulsion, enrollment in special education, or alternative school placement (McDougal & Chafouleas, 2005). Martens, Witt, Daly, and Vollmer (1999) state that the ethical benefits of FBA outweigh the costs, particularly when one considers the time usually spent on ineffective interventions or interventions that might inadvertently strengthen a problem behavior (e.g., suspension). Ethically, FBA should be considered for use whenever negative behavior is impeding a student's learning or the learning of others.

Overview of the FBA Process

Although the methods for engaging in functional assessment vary, FBA usually involves a four-step process:

1. Problem identification

2. Problem investigation and analysis

3. Intervention plan development and implementation

4. Intervention plan evaluation

This process is a logical sequence for making decisions about what the problem behaviors are and how they can be changed. First, the practitioner must clearly and specifically identify the problem, and when multiple problems are evident, decide which ones will be the initial focus of change.

The practitioner should next investigate and analyze the chosen target behavior by examining the contexts in which it occurs and the variables that predict or influence the behavior. Part of investigation and analysis is identifying a positive alternative behavior that serves the same function for the student as the less desirable behavior. For example, let's assume that a student's problem behavior is repeatedly getting out of her seat to sharpen her pencil during math class. If it is determined that she does this because the math work is too hard for her, a number of interventions automatically come to mind: She could be given extra help so she becomes able to do the task, the task could be made easier so she could be successful independently, or she could be given several sharp pencils prior to math class. This student could also be instructed in the use of a cue (e.g., raising her hand) to solicit teacher support and assistance during independent seatwork in math.

As this example illustrates, the two initial stages—problem identification and problem investigation and analysis—are critical in order to move successfully to intervention plan development and implementation. The FBA assessment process directly informs intervention plan development and implementation.

Finally, during the last step in the process, evaluation, the plan is monitored and formatively revised on the basis of student progress.

The specifics of FBAs and intervention plans are explored further in the next five chapters of this volume. Meanwhile, Table 1.1 gives an overview of the complete process.

TABLE 1.1

Stages in the FBA Process

Stage 1: Problem Identification

- Collect background information.
- List behaviors that interfere with student progress.
- Prioritize behaviors on the list and select one or two behaviors as initial targets of change.
- Define each target behavior in clear and specific terms.
- Collect information about the current level of each behavior (obtain baseline information).

Stage 2: Problem Investigation and Analysis

- Identify conditions that predict the behavior.
- Identify skill deficits and communicative intent.
- Develop a functional theory (hypothesis) about why the behavior occurs.
- Identify strengths, interests, and potential replacement behaviors.

Stage 3: Intervention Plan Development and Implementation

- Link assessment to intervention.
- Select an intervention technique.
- Develop the behavior intervention plan and begin implementation.

Stage 4: Intervention Plan Evaluation

- Assess intervention integrity.
- Collect and graph progress monitoring results.
- Conduct formative assessment.
- Conduct summative assessment.

Multicultural Issues in the Use of Functional Behavioral Assessment

For an assessment tool to be truly valuable, it must have utility across ages, situations, and groups, including culturally varied groups. Although the cultural relevancy of behavioral assessment and intervention procedures has not been as controversial a subject as has standardized testing, the techniques of FBA do require the practitioner to study behavior in one setting (the school) and then make judgments about the behavior's severity and the conditions surrounding it. Interpretations of behavior, and what should be done about behavior, are influenced by cultural factors (see Ramirez, Lepage, Kratochwill, & Duffy, 1998). In fact, cultural responsiveness (e.g., interest in and knowledge of a client's culture) has been shown to lead to increased client satisfaction during counseling (Atkinson & Lowe, 1995).

Ingraham (2000) provides a useful multicultural framework for conceptualizing the consultation process in a school. She suggests that the consultant—the person working with the teacher or parent in the FBA process—must understand his or her own culture, recognize the effect of that culture on others, and possess knowledge and respect for the cultures of others. For example, it is important to recognize that the problem definition and acceptable strategies to reduce disruptive or disrespectful behavior may differ significantly among European American, African American, and Hispanic or Latin American populations. Thus, although effective assessment and intervention approaches might be identified, they may need to be tailored to be acceptable to the culture of the child, family, and community. It has been theorized that the multiculturally proficient practitioner should possess the following competencies: "(a) understanding the impact of one's race/ethnicity and culture, (b) valuing and understanding the impact of other races/ethnicities and cultures, (c) adapting a culturally responsive consultation style, and (d) adapting culturally responsive strategies during the problem solving stages" (Ramirez et al., 1998, p. 484).

Developing multicultural competency is likely to be an ongoing and active learning process, during which practitioners continually improve their skills. For a more detailed review of multicultural considerations in school consultation, see Ingraham (2000) and Ramirez et al. (1998).

Limitations of Functional Behavioral Assessment

Although we have described several reasons for engaging in an FBA, limitations on its use also have been identified. One concern frequently raised by theorists, researchers, and practitioners centers on the labor intensiveness of the process. Some observers suggest that FBA may best be reserved for use with students who demonstrate severe classroom difficulties. Caution also has been voiced that little research to date has been conducted with students possessing mild disabilities or behavior problems, making it difficult to verify that the benefits of engaging in the FBA process outweigh the costs in terms of time and energy. Braden and

Kratochwill (1997) have suggested that a functional behavioral assessment may not always be necessary to intervene effectively. For example, if there is a high likelihood that an intervention will work with varying problem behaviors, or if the cost of assessment exceeds intervention benefits, then it might be acceptable to try an intervention without first conducting a functional assessment.

In addition, some theorists suggest that FBA fails to look beyond observable behavior to understand how complex individual histories and contexts interact to influence a child's actions. Some assessment models have placed little emphasis on factors such as temperament, medication use, history of abuse, family relationships, and parenting practices. In response, more comprehensive behavioral and ecological approaches have been developed to identify and intervene with factors within the individual and variables in the home or community environments that may be supporting the challenging behavior.

Finally, questions also remain about the FBA process itself. Little is yet known about whether indirect, informant methods of gathering FBA information are sufficiently accurate compared with more direct methods, such as experimental analysis (i.e., systematically exposing the student to various conditions to determine an intervention's effectiveness). In addition, as Gresham, Watson, and Skinner (2001) have stated, classrooms are complex environments in which it may be difficult, even with training, to identify accurately what is influencing or reinforcing a behavior. Thus, although FBA can be a useful and powerful tool in many situations, it has its limitations.

Putting It All Together

The FBA process involves steps for identifying and analyzing behavior problems and finding solutions to those problems. Throughout the process, behavior is seen as occurring for specific reasons, and plans for change are developed with those reasons in mind. These plans focus on teaching and supporting more appropriate behaviors, which serve the same function for the student, and on modifying the predictive conditions that exist in the student's environment. Despite various unanswered questions about the use of FBA, current literature generally supports it as a method of reducing challenging behaviors (Heckman, Conroy, Fox, & Chait, 2000; McDougal, Nastasi, & Chafouleas, 2005; Repp, 1994).

The practical, legal, and ethical reasons we have outlined in support of FBA suggest that it should be a part of any practitioner's knowledge base. FBA provides a practical problem-solving framework for assessment, tied to intervention that promotes good practice. This endorsement does not imply support for the use of comprehensive FBA for every problem; it may not fit or be applicable in every situation. Rather, we consider FBA to be a valuable decision-making process, in which methods should be modified to match needs and resources in the particular situation.

CHAPTER 2

Getting Ready for Functional Behavioral Assessment: Thinking about Influences on Behavior

Joey, the first grader we met in chapter 1, is at risk for demonstrating problem behaviors for several reasons. An assessment that considers his individual characteristics, his family system (including extended family), and cultural influences reveals that Joey possesses weak academic skills, reacts poorly to verbal redirection and physical cues, is from a family with few financial resources, and has encountered inconsistent adult structure and support. He has been placed in a classroom where teacher feedback comes primarily in the form of telling students what not to do, and most of the instruction is given in large groups, with limited feedback to individual children. Joey's independent work on tasks requiring reading and writing suggests that he typically performs slowly and often misses up to 50 percent of assigned questions. Finally, Joey's aunt, with whom he lives, has had little contact with the school system and has been slow to return calls from the school related to Joey's misbehavior.

Joey's history suggests inconsistent experiences with adults—most dramatically, physical abuse and abandonment by his mother. Accommodations at school appear needed to help him cope with these experiences. In addition, a closer and more positive collaboration between the school and Joey's aunt could involve teaching him prosocial replacement behaviors and support him in using such behaviors in both settings, while also providing a more comprehensive approach to dealing with his challenging behaviors in the classroom.

When classroom-based antecedents and reasons for challenging behavior are fairly straightforward, FBA may focus solely on factors in close proximity to the problem behavior. However, using the principles of FBA with a diverse school population requires consideration of factors outside the typical antecedent-behavior-consequence (ABC) paradigm (e.g., Quinn & McDougal, 1998). More complex cases, such as Joey's, require a thorough FBA that takes a multifaceted approach, examining factors that (a) are subject to manipulation or change via the intervention plan and (b) influence behavior but are not easily changed and therefore require accommodation. An example of the latter factor is a child who exhibits behavior problems in school related to ongoing verbal altercations between his parents. Although school personnel cannot resolve the unrest in the child's home, they can greet this student at the door each morning and steer him toward a supportive staff member when needed. The accommodation of easing the student's morning transition into the school setting may prevent a behavioral episode.

In this chapter, we begin with a brief review of individual factors that may affect student behavior; this review is followed by discussion of the larger contextual influences of family and culture. Because our primary audience is the school-based practitioner, we outline some classroom strategies that may effectively accommodate diverse students. Our main focus in this book is assessing and intervening with specific student behaviors; however, it is important to address certain issues that inform the process. Having said this, it is important to note that this chapter does not encompass all the factors that may affect an individual's behavior—it is simply a reminder to consider multiple factors in any student assessment.

Individual Factors Affecting Behavior

Individual factors that may affect behavior include learning problems, self-efficacy and motivation, and physiology.

Learning Problems

Learning problems and behavioral difficulties have often been reported to co-occur (Rock, Fessler, & Church, 1997; Rosenberg, 1997; Witt, Daly, & Noell, 2000). Rock et al. have suggested that students who have both learning and behavioral problems benefit less from special education services and are at greater risk of dropping out of school and having continuing problems into adulthood. In addition, children who experience learning problems are at greater risk of showing symptoms associated with depression, are poor problem solvers, have a lowered sense of worth and competence, and are generally less actively involved learners (Waterman, 2002). Thus, in addition to intense and focused academic intervention, students with learning problems may require behavioral support.

Self-Efficacy and Motivation

Self-efficacy and motivation influence a child's success. A child who experiences multiple failures, socially or academically, is apt to have low motivation and is more at risk for behavioral problems (Mercer & Mercer, 1998). Motivation is related to self-efficacy because, in order to be motivated to perform a task, a student must first perceive that she has the skills and abilities required to be successful. According to Bruning, Schraw, and Ronning (1995), cited in Pajares (1996):

> Self-efficacy is strongly related to critical classroom variables such as task engagement, persistence, strategy use, help seeking, and task performance. High self-efficacy is also associated with greater flexibility, resistance to negative feedback, improved academic performance, and the use of desired strategies among students. (p. 131)

The literature suggests that students develop this positive sense of self-efficacy through positive feedback received for their accomplishments. Therefore, in addition to curricular interventions, it may be important to enhance students' perceptions of and beliefs about their abilities.

Physiology

Myriad biological issues can affect a child's cognitive, social, emotional, and behavioral development. For example, prematurity, lead poisoning, and poor nutrition are related to learning, attention, and language disorders (Cherkes-Julkowski, 1998). Attention deficit disorder (Copps, 1992), alcoholism and drug abuse (Crabbe, McSwigan, & Kelknap, 1985), schizophrenia (Paul, 1980), and learning disabilities (Alarcón, DeFries, Ligh, & Pennington, 1997) may, at least in part, be inherited. Children with these types of medical and physiological issues may require medical treatment and specialized interventions in addition to behavioral support. Continued student progress monitoring inherent in the FBA/BIP process can be useful in evaluating the combined effects of intervention strategies integrating medical, behavioral, and other specialized strategies.

Contextual Factors Affecting Behavior

Factors that affect behaviors may be related to the multiple contexts that influence the child. Among the most prominent contextual factors are those related to the family and the school. Other factors concern peer relationships and cultural influences.

Family-Based Factors

Poverty, family composition, and family interaction all affect children's behavior.

Poverty. Ramey and Ramey (1998) and McLoyd (1998) report that poverty is often associated with poor health care and nutrition, reduced self-efficacy, and diminished educational and vocational opportunities. Delays in language development, lowered expectations for success, passivity or apathy, higher school dropout rates, and lowered achievement have all been found to have a relationship with poverty.

Family composition. Children who live in single-parent homes or have very young single mothers may be at risk for learning or behavioral problems. Bronfenbrenner (1970) found that children with absent fathers had lower achievement motivation, lower self-esteem, and greater difficulties delaying gratification than did children whose fathers were present. These children were also more vulnerable to group influences. Very young mothers were found to be under considerable stress (Prater, 1992), potentially affecting the learning and behavior of both the mother and the child.

Family interaction. The style or manner in which parents interact with their children also may affect learning and behavior. Children from families that are "underorganized" or chaotic may have difficulty attending to school tasks and may be disruptive in class. Children from "overorganized" families—that is, with parents who are overly involved or protective—may demonstrate greater anxiety or oppositional behaviors than their peers (Green, 1992).

Verbal and physical abuse or neglect contributes to learning and behavioral difficulties as well. Children who suffer abuse or neglect may be either more aggressive or more compliant than their peers (Crittenden, 1989), have lower self-esteem, show greater evidence of psychological disorders, and have interpersonal difficulties (Mullen, Martin, Anderson, Romans, & Herbison, 1996).

School-Based Factors

A number of classroom variables have been found to affect student development. Poor instruction or a lack of instruction clearly affects a child's academic, social, or behavioral growth. Christenson, Ysseldyke, and Thurlow (1989) have suggested that children learn better in classrooms that are positive and supportive. These authors report that teachers who are encouraging, have positive expectations, and are cheerful and enthusiastic create an environment conducive to effective learning. Sprick (1985) also found that teachers who attend to positive rather than negative classroom events improve both the behavior and achievement of their students. Other characteristics found to create a positive classroom environment are realistic expectations for learning, age-appropriate instruction, direct questioning, use of reinforcers for appropriate academic and social behaviors, active tracking of student progress, prompting, and seeing errors as a natural part of learning.

Carroll's (1963) model of school learning provides a succinct overview of the multiple school-based influences on student outcomes. This model is presented in Figure 2.1. Carroll's model acknowledges the individual differences that students bring to the classroom, yet also recognizes the impact of classroom variables on student outcomes. As Ysseldyke and Elliott (1999) have stated, acknowledgment of the importance of the instructional ecology requires a problem-solving orientation to assessment that takes the multiple influences on student learning into consideration.

Peer Relationships

Students with learning or behavioral problems frequently have lower social status and experience difficulty in social interactions (Handwerk & Marshall, 1998; Smith, 1995). Many of these students also have been found to have lower social acceptance than their peers without these disabilities (Bauer, Keefe, & Shea, 2001). When students with learning or behavioral problems are seen as less mature than their peers, this also appears to contribute to feelings of isolation and loneliness (Tur-Kaspa, Wesel, & Segev, 1998). Children with learning problems tend to have less hope that their feelings of loneliness or isolation will change in the future.

Cultural Influences

Cultural, racial, or ethnic differences between school personnel and the child and his family may interfere with school and family communication, as well as with intervention development and implementation. Given the importance of parental participation in children's schooling (Dauber & Epstein, 1993), misunderstandings between the family and school personnel because of cultural, ethnic, or

FIGURE 2.1

Carroll's Model of School Learning

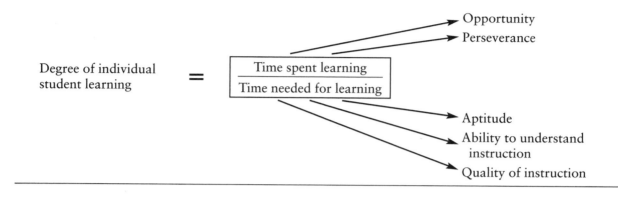

language differences may place a child at greater risk for learning or behavioral struggles.

Intervening for Change

As the preceding discussion suggests, a number of individual and contextual factors affect a child's behavior. Although educators cannot significantly influence all the factors that underlie problem behavior, they can have a positive impact on many of them—such as how a child learns and the child's beliefs about and motivation to learn. Chapters 8, 9, and 10 outline specific intervention ideas and activities that can improve children's learning and behavior. The remainder of this chapter reviews the literature on designing effective classroom environments to promote positive academic behavior.

Effective Classrooms

To implement a problem-solving model to assess student learning, we first must have a basic understanding of what effective instructional environments look like. As researchers have attempted to delineate the components of effective instruction (see Blair, 1984; Good & Brophy, 1984), a number of categories have consistently emerged. Effective instructional environments are characterized by high student engagement, frequent instructional review and feedback opportunities, appropriate instructional match, a well-organized schedule, minimization of academic downtime, and practice activities to increase student success.

Gettinger and Stoiber (1999) provide an excellent summary of data relating to effective teaching. These authors group teaching behaviors into four categories: academic learning time, focus and clarity, difficulty level, and feedback. Definitions and examples of each type are compiled in Table 2.1.

Characteristics of Effective Instructional Environments

Teaching Behavior	*Definition*	*Example*
Academic learning time	The amount of time provided for teaching/learning The degree to which students are on-task or actively involved The amount of time students spend successfully in meaningful tasks	Moving around the class Relying on routines Limiting transition and other noninstructional downtime Providing material of appropriate difficulty Providing material that is interesting Using different instructional formats, such as cooperative groups
Focus and clarity	Organization of content, communication of expectations, teacher familiarity with material, questioning strategies used Teaching that is oriented toward maximizing opportunity to learn	Offering step-by-step explanations Applying content Linking ideas between lessons Asking critical thinking questions
Difficulty level	Appropriate instructional match to ensure moderate to high rates of success	Good understanding by students, few errors made
Feedback	Information about accuracy and correction or reteaching if needed	Giving frequent and specific feedback Initial practice with high rates of success Teaching to mastery Reviewing daily Reviewing weekly or monthly

The process of learning, or going from beginning skill level to mastery, involves a sequence of steps no matter what the task to be learned. This sequence has been referred to as the *instructional hierarchy* (Daly, Lentz, & Boyer, 1996). Each step in the learning process corresponds to a different set of instructional principles designed to promote mastery of that step and movement to the next. Determining a student's level of skill development, or stage in the learning process, allows for easy identification of corresponding instructional principles that may be used to identify, create, or modify a specific task. A number of academic intervention ideas based on the instructional hierarchy are presented in chapter 7.

As shown in Figure 2.2, the stages of the instructional hierarchy following effective instruction are developing accuracy (acquisition), developing fluency, and generalizing skills (Daly, Witt, Martens, & Dool, 1997). Most of an educator's attention and resources are dedicated to accuracy and fluency because students are most likely to encounter difficulty in the beginning stages of skill development.

In the *accurate performance* stage, a student learns to perform accurately but is not yet fluent or automatic in performing. Instructional strategies at this stage include teaching the skill and then facilitating correct performance by modeling, prompting the student to perform, and providing error correction and positive feedback.

Fluency refers to a student's accurate and rapid performance of a skill or task. Fluency is often measured by rate (e.g., how fast a child can read a text) or duration/latency (e.g., how long before the child answers a question). Teaching strategies at this stage include plenty of drill and practice, as well as reinforcement for correct performance.

Generalization occurs when the student is able to perform the behavior accurately and quickly in novel situations, in other settings, or at a later time. For example, students can apply their reading skills to math word problems. Teaching strategies here emphasize practicing the skill under natural conditions (in different settings and at different times) and incorporating a variety of novel conditions in the practice.

Beyond this schema, *adaptation* occurs when a student is able to modify the skill to meet new demands (e.g., computing sales tax at the grocery store). Adaptation is often taught through simulated problem solving.

Worksheet 2.1, at the end of this chapter, lists some key classroom variables and school-home connections to consider when conducting an FBA. On a more global level, there are a number of well-developed formats to assist in the evaluation of an instructional environment—for example, the Instructional Environment Scale–II (Ysseldyke & Christenson, 1993) and the Ecobehavioral Assessment System Software (Greenwood & Carta, 1994). Although these are certainly useful tools, they can be time-consuming to administer and are not practical in all situations.

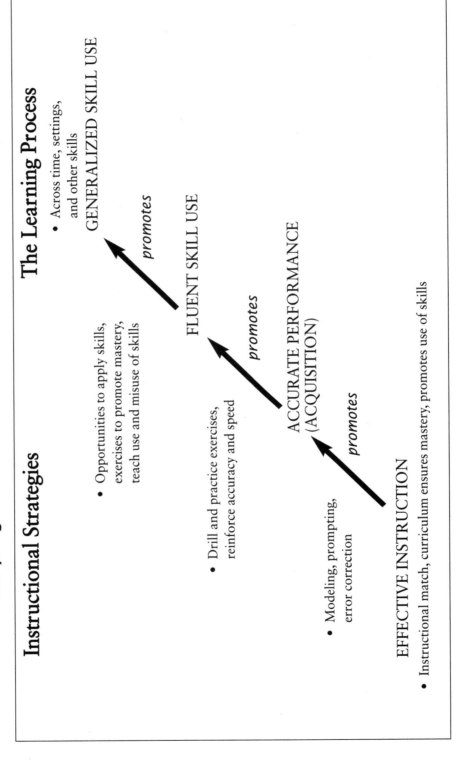

FIGURE 2.2

Analyzing Academic Problems: The Instructional Hierarchy

Effective Schoolwide Systems

The larger school environment can also significantly affect student behavior. School environments characterized by loud and chaotic hallway transitions, poorly supervised common areas, a lack of clear behavioral expectations, and inconsistent disciplinary procedures are likely to host more challenging student behavior than schools in which these conditions do not exist. Problem behavior and the interventions developed to alter it take place in the context of the larger school system. Therefore, positive behavior should be promoted at the system level.

Sugai, Sprague, Horner, and Walker (2000) and others (Crone & Horner, 2000; Lewis & Sugai, 1999) have identified a number of critical factors to consider in developing effective, positive schoolwide support systems. An effective behavioral support system (EBSS) should provide strategies for promoting positive behavior and preventing problems among the student body as a whole (universal interventions) and among those students who are at risk for developing behavioral problems (targeted at-risk group interventions). It should also provide strategies for ameliorating behavioral problems that a small group of students already exhibit (indicated or individualized interventions). Thus the EBSS should involve academic and behavioral goals that are both preventative and remedial. It must also provide consistent support across ages, grades, and cultural groups, and identify and establish links between the school and the community. It requires input from administrators, counselors, special educators, school psychologists, teachers, parents, and students. A team approach is helpful in creating a sustainable and resilient management system and in creating an organization that has a variety of skills and strengths. An EBSS also requires procedures for the sharing of information, eliciting information from the larger school and community environments, and solving complex problems (Todd, Horner, Sugai, & Colvin, 1999).

The Office of Special Education Programs Center on Positive Behavioral Interventions (Sugai et al., 2000) emphasizes that interventions developed at any of the three levels—universal, targeted, or indicated—need to be practical, sensitive to social and cultural values, and sustainable. Because challenging student behaviors are largely influenced by environmental factors, intervening first at the school level may be the most economical approach for decreasing the behavior across diverse populations of students. A schoolwide system requires that, for particularly challenging students, functional behavioral assessments and interventions be developed, monitored, and evaluated over time. In addition, individualized plans are likely to be more effective and more easily implemented when the school as a whole has consistent expectations, discipline, and strategies for promoting positive student behavior.

An effective schoolwide system should also give serious consideration to the children's cultural contexts. The Council for Children with Behavioral Disorders Task Force for Cultural Issues (Bauer et al., 2001) offers the following guidelines for providing appropriate services to diverse groups of students:

1. Ensure that students from diverse cultures are truly exhibiting emotional/behavioral disorders rather than culturally based behavior.

2. Provide respectful, culturally appropriate services.

3. Implement culturally and linguistically competent assessment procedures.

4. Recruit professionals of various cultural, ethnic, and linguistic groups.

5. Provide preservice and inservice training to professionals in modifications of practice that better address the characteristics of students with emotional/behavioral disorders who are from various cultural, ethnic, or linguistic groups.

6. Create a welcoming climate where students from various cultural, ethnic, and linguistic groups feel valued, respected, and physically and psychologically safe.

7. Enhance the cultural knowledge base of professionals, clients/students, and the public at large.

Practitioners who have received diversity training and have cultural sensitivity are best able to achieve these seven goals.

Effective School-Home Connections

Although the instructional context certainly plays a large role in learning, to understand the multiple influences on individual functioning, other contexts should also be considered. Certainly, the home environment is one of the greatest influences on a child's functioning, and the need for a connection between home and school becomes clear when we examine estimates of the large amount of time students are not in school. Time spent outside of school between birth and age 18 has been estimated at 87 to 91 percent of a child's total time (Christenson & Buerkle, 1999). We also know that the actions families take to support learning, such as establishing a consistent routine and discussing homework, are more important indicators of student outcome than are descriptive or status variables, such as income level (Dauber & Epstein, 1993).

In a review of articles exploring family factors that influence student achievement, Christenson, Rounds, and Gorney (1992) found five important factors that may be altered through intervention: parental expectations and attributions, structure for learning, home affective environment, disciplinary orientation, and parent participation in education. These factors, along with examples of each, are described in Table 2.2.

The literature clearly demonstrates the need to consider family influences on student learning and to view families as potential partners in influencing children's learning. Christenson, Rounds, and Gorney (1992) recommended that one good way to do this is to consider student learning to be a responsibility that is shared between home and school and to adopt a nontraditional view of parent involvement. A nontraditional view involves expanding the scope of parental involvement,

TABLE 2.2

Changeable Family Factors Influencing Student Achievement

Family Factor	Example
Parental expectations and attributions	High, realistic expectations for performance
	Positive encouragement for efforts
Structure for learning	Modeling of reading and presence of reading materials
	Schedule for homework completion
	Monitoring television viewing
Home affective environment	Parental acceptance and encouragement
	Parental nurturance of and concern for child's developmental needs
Disciplinary orientation	Setting and enforcing clear standards/rules
	Encouraging discussion and independence
Parental participation in education	Involvement in learning activities at home, such as homework and responding to school notes
	Involvement in school activities, such as attending meetings and volunteering

extending opportunities for connections, and increasing communication between school and home. In fact, in Epstein's (1995) spheres of influence model, the goal is to push the two spheres—the home and school settings—closer together in order to increase interactions and shared responsibility. The literature points to the need for congruent messages between home and school. Therefore, the match between home and school expectations for student learning should be examined (Christenson & Buerkle, 1999), with an emphasis on finding ways to strengthen communication between home and school.

Despite all this evidence, we acknowledge that some parents and schools are unable, do not know how, or for other reasons find it challenging to establish a strong school-home connection. The reasons for this impasse are beyond the scope of this chapter and may require significant systemwide efforts to resolve. Still, it is important to explore issues related to the home and school connection when conducting an FBA. The examiner may be able to determine that a lack of school-home communication and involvement is linked to the FBA referral or to the problem behaviors the child is manifesting. If a system needs modification and such modification does not take place, then it is likely that the same problem will occur in the future. Efforts made at this point may prevent a future need to spend resources addressing a similar problem. If ineffective school-home communication is identified as a factor, then attempts to address it may be undertaken. These contacts may include the use of daily or weekly notes or reports of behavior.

Putting It All Together

Educators can point to an environment external to the school, such as the home or community, as fostering a student's problem behavior. Even if the best efforts to help change that environment have met with significant resistance, it does not mean that nothing further can be done. Rather, the problem may need to be rethought to determine what parts of the environment might be changed and what methods could be used to implement that change. Rather than focus on functional behavioral assessment as a process to solve a child's problem in a specific environment, we have suggested in this chapter that the practitioner consider multiple aspects of the child's world, including factors unique to the child (e.g., cognitive ability and sense of self-efficacy) and factors that exist in the home, community, and school environments (including cultural features, peer interaction, parental support, and instructional methods) as potential areas for assessment and intervention. Such a comprehensive assessment allows for the reconceptualization of the problem and promotes development of multiple, indirect, and creative solutions. This view of the problem is consistent with the overriding goal of functional behavioral assessment: to determine which factors initiate and sustain a problem behavior and to engage in an ongoing search for effective interventions. Although there are many areas in which educators have little power to make effective changes, the good news is that there are also many places where they do.

Instructional Environment and School-Home Connections

Instructional Environment	Notes
1. How much time is dedicated to learning, and to what degree are the students actively involved?	
2. Are expectations clearly communicated, and is content well organized?	
3. How is the difficulty level of material decided for each student? Is there an appropriate instructional match?	
4. How is feedback on performance provided?	
School-Home Connections	
5. What options are available for parent involvement at school? Are those options utilized?	
6. How is information communicated between home and school?	
7. What is the "match" between parent and school expectations?	
8. How is the home environment structured for learning? How does the school communicate information about developing that structure?	

From *Functional Behavioral Assessment and Intervention in Schools: A Practitioner's Guide (Grades 1–8)*, by J. L. McDougal, S. M. Chafouleas, and B. Waterman, 2006, Champaign, IL: Research Press (800-519-2707; www.researchpress.com)

CHAPTER 3

Problem Identification

Joey's teacher has met with the school psychologist to conduct an FBA and develop a behavior intervention plan (BIP). In the meantime, because of his background and family history, Joey also has been referred to the school counselor for support and to the school social worker, who makes periodic home visits. In the initial FBA meeting, the teacher relays numerous concerns about Joey, ranging from his tantrums and disruptive behavior to noncompliance and poor academic skills. From these behaviors, tantrums (episodes of dropping to the floor, yelling, crying, and hitting, kicking, spitting, or throwing) and noncompliance (failing to follow individually issued teacher directions within 10 seconds) are selected as target behaviors. The selection is made because the tantrums represent a safety issue in the classroom, and the noncompliance often is the precursor to the tantrums. Documentation of the tantrums indicates that, on average, they occur three times per week, lasting 12 minutes, with generally high intensity (physical aggression is typically present). Compliance with teacher requests is assessed with a daily behavior report card (DBRC), completed by the teacher twice a day. Joey earns an average compliance rating of 1.3 on a 5-point scale (in the poor range). Therefore, decreasing the current frequency, intensity, and duration of tantrums and increasing compliance ratings become the focus of intervention.

In this chapter, we begin looking at the actual FBA process, with a discussion of the first stage: problem identification. Problem identification is perhaps the most critical part of the entire process. If the problem behavior is not clearly defined in a way that can be measured (i.e., operationalized), then the rest of the FBA process will break down. In fact, it has been suggested that the best predictor of successful problem resolution is the extent to which the problem is initially defined in concrete, measurable terms (Bergan & Tombari, 1975, 1976).

Usually, problem identification begins with interviews with educators, parents, and the student in order to generate a list of behaviors that interfere with the student's ability to succeed in school. This process is best informed by objective direct observation, which generally helps to clarify and quantify behavioral challenges. Behaviors on this list are then prioritized, and one or two target behaviors are selected, clearly defined, and measured in the classroom context. Finally, a problem identification statement is generated for each target behavior. This statement includes an operational definition of the behavior and a baseline measurement.

Appendix A includes the complete Functional Behavioral Assessment Worksheet, which guides the entire FBA process; Table 3.1 lists the four stages in the process,

TABLE 3.1

Stage 1: Problem Identification

Stage 1: Problem Identification

- Collect background information.
- List behaviors that interfere with student progress.
- Prioritize behaviors on the list and select one or two behaviors as initial targets of change.
- Define each target behavior in clear and specific terms.
- Collect information about the current level of each behavior (obtain baseline information).

Stage 2: Problem Investigation and Analysis

Stage 3: Intervention Plan Development and Implementation

Stage 4: Intervention Plan Evaluation

detailing the specific tasks to be accomplished during the problem identification stage.

The limited amount of space on the FBA Worksheet does not allow description of the big picture—the scope of all problem behaviors the student might exhibit. Instead, the form is designed to help practitioners focus on one or two well-defined problems that the intervention will eventually target, assess the impact of distant factors that may influence these problem behaviors, and list smaller behaviors that are seen as precursors. This portion of the form is shown in Figure 3.1.

Collect Background Information

Collecting relevant but concise background information is an important first step in problem identification. Reviewing records; conducting teacher, parent, and student interviews; and consulting with school staff and community members may help identify challenging behaviors that occur across settings and assist in prioritizing targets for behavioral change. Collecting too much information, however, is not time-efficient and can cause confusion about the purpose of the FBA. For example, spending significant time detailing a student's family structure or documenting movement through various school districts (if the child has moved often) does not keep the focus on presenting problems. It may suffice to state that the student's background includes a number of familial and school transitions and adjustments. However, if the presenting problem can be directly related to recent transitions at home or school (e.g., a teacher's going on maternity leave, parental separation), then it is wise to explore this information in some detail.

FIGURE 3.1

FBA Worksheet: Problem Identification

Student _____ Grade _____ Date _____

Referral source _____ Evaluator _____

Identify and define up to two target behaviors that most interfere with the child's functioning in the classroom. Assess or directly observe the frequency (how often), intensity (high, medium, low), and duration of each.

BEHAVIOR(S)	Frequency	Intensity	Duration

Collecting relevant background information is also important for identifying *distant predictors* of challenging school behavior—also known as *distal setting events*—events that influence negative behavior but are removed in time and place from the behavior's actual occurrence (Gresham, Watson, & Skinner, 2001; O'Neill, Horner, Albin, Sprague, Storey, & Newton, 1997). In their discussion of setting events, Gresham et al. provide an excellent example in which a child's noncompliant classroom behavior was related to getting into a fight on the bus on the way to school. If the FBA found, for example, that a stepparent in the home does not agree with medication for the child's attention-deficit/hyperactivity disorder and refuses to give the medication in the morning, this would be important to know when targeting that child's recent disruptive classroom behavior. Chapter 2 discussed several distant predictors that might also influence a student's behavior, such as physiology or family factors. At the problem identification stage, distant predictors are used to prioritize and select behavioral targets (e.g., a discussion of medication compliance for the child in the previous example). In chapter 4, which discusses problem investigation and analysis, these predictors will be assessed in more depth.

In summary, when collecting background information, it is important to find the appropriate balance between the relevant and the irrelevant. With the right balance, the information will lead to a more complete understanding of the student than will an assessment based only on an antecedent-behavior-consequence (ABC) model, which may consider only the relationship between the current environment and behavior. In order to achieve a balance between too much and too little, ask, "How is this information useful in solving the current problem?" If the answer is not clear, then it is probably time to move on, acknowledge the information in a summary statement, and steer further discussion more directly toward the problem area.

List Target Behaviors

Although identifying problems may seem a simple task, there are actually many common pitfalls, such as not being specific enough so that change can be measured, identifying and trying to tackle too many problems at once, and not selecting a reasonable goal. Complicating the picture even more, the FBA process is usually carried out by several different people, who may all come to the process with varying backgrounds and perspectives.

Usually, problem identification begins with the referring source, and information about the problem is collected during an interview with that person. However, the problem descriptions provided by referring sources are sometimes too vague or general to lead clearly to useful interventions (see Lambert, 1976). Further, many referrals involve numerous problem behaviors that need to be narrowed down to one or two reasonable targets for change. Thus the consultant in such a situation faces the task of listing the referral concerns being brought forth, sorting out relevant information, and prioritizing problem behaviors.

First, the relevant background information should be summarized and the problem areas discussed. In the school, a team is usually involved in this phase of the process, with participation from the classroom teacher or teachers; parents; school psychologist, social worker, and administrator; and, if it is developmentally appropriate, the student. The point of the discussion is to develop a list of potential target behaviors, with the understanding that the behaviors on the list must be prioritized and that only one or two can be selected for intervention. The selection process is somewhat subjective because the identified problems are often those that most bother the adults working with the child or those believed to interfere most with the child's ability to function in the classroom. Caution is needed here because modifying these behaviors may not always serve the best interests of the child. For example, fighting on the playground is generally unacceptable in school and would be a worthy target for intervention. But if a student's fighting is related to bullying, intimidation, or physical harassment by other students, then these factors also would have to be addressed in order for the ensuing intervention to be effective and in the child's best interest.

Select Target Behaviors

A key concept to keep in mind during the selection process is that of social validity, which has to do with considerations about what is important to society, consumer satisfaction, and the appropriateness of the intervention in a given setting (Wolf, 1978). During problem identification, what this boils down to is a need to understand how the referral source, the student, and other significant adults perceive the problem and to work to incorporate their concerns into the identification of target behaviors and intervention planning. It is easy to see why schools often take a team approach in assessing and intervening to change challenging student behavior. This

TABLE 3.2

Characteristics of Potential Target Behaviors

1. May result in physical harm to self or others.
2. May become more serious if not modified.
3. Are most distressing to the parent or teacher (by rank order).
4. Persistently disrupt or interfere with instruction.
5. Are precursors to other, more serious problem behaviors.
6. Are deemed important by the child or the child's family.
7. Deviate most from age norms for the child.
8. Significantly interfere with student's academic progress or daily functioning.

approach is more likely to achieve the commitment—acceptance and investment—needed to define and change the problem.

In general, the referral source or those responsible for implementing the designed interventions drive the identification and prioritization of target behaviors. However, we do have some recommendations to guide that selection process. For example, as already noted, if a behavior has significant potential to harm the child or others, that behavior would likely need to be targeted first. Table 3.2—based on the work of Alessi (1988), Meyer and Evans (1989), and Demchak (1993)—presents other suggestions for selecting and prioritizing target behaviors.

In addition to the considerations noted in Table 3.2, there also must be some consideration of replacement behaviors and intervention goals. The target behaviors selected will later be used to identify replacement behaviors and positively stated intervention goals. For this reason, practitioners may choose to define and measure positive target behaviors. For instance, it may be helpful to assess rates of compliance as opposed to incidents of noncompliance and to document on-task behavior as opposed to levels of out-of-seat or off-task behavior. Focusing on one positive behavior may also effectively target several negative behaviors (e.g., assessing time on task as opposed to time off task, out of seat, and bothering peers). We address the identification of replacement behaviors and setting intervention goals in subsequent chapters. However, we encourage practitioners to consider these factors now to aid in the identification and definition of target behaviors that may more easily translate into practical intervention goals and teachable replacement behaviors.

Finally, when selecting target behaviors it is necessary to assess for the presence of *precursor behaviors* in hypothesized *behavior chains*. A precursor behavior is a smaller, less intense behavior that often occurs before larger, more intense behavioral episodes. For example, physical confrontations between two students might be traced back to name-calling or teasing by one of them. In this case, the name-calling may be an important behavior to target because it precedes the physical confrontation. If precursor behaviors or behavior chains can be identified, then it is generally appropriate to amend the identified problems to include both the smaller precursor behaviors and the more intense episodes. These factors are discussed fully in chapter 4.

At this point in the problem identification stage, up to two target behaviors should have been selected, based on prioritization of problem areas and consideration of replacement behaviors, intervention goals, and potential behavior chains. Now each target behavior needs to be clearly defined in objective, measurable terms to allow for the collection of baseline information.

Define Target Behaviors

A good problem definition, or one that is *operationalized*, allows specific intervention ideas to be generated based on that definition. For example, if Petey is described as "getting into trouble on the playground," we have no idea what kind of behavior he is exhibiting or what is happening as a result of the behavior. Is Petey hitting his peers, refusing to share the swing, not following the rule about walking instead of running in designated areas, or all of the above? If, instead, we are told that "Petey does not follow the rules for playing tag on the playground, often pushing students to the ground when tagging them," we have identified a specific problem. This specific definition allows us to investigate this behavior to see if it occurs only on the playground, to see if others are engaging in similar behavior, and to measure accurately the occurrence of Petey's pushing behavior. With a clear definition of the problem behavior, it is much easier to focus on an appropriate intervention. For example, if it is observed that other peers also push when playing tag, it may be decided that the whole class could benefit from instruction in the rules and a referee for tag games in order to eliminate the problem.

In another example, let's say that third grader Cindy is described as not being able to read. From that description, we know at least that the problem falls in the academic area of reading; we now need to define more clearly the scope of the problem. For example, can she really read nothing at all? If we find that Cindy is reading at a first-grade level (two years behind her peers) and that she knows a limited number of basic sight words but is having trouble grasping letter-sound correspondences, we are on the right track toward intervention. Additional examples of high- and low-quality problem definitions are shown in Table 3.3. High-quality definitions assist intervention planning, whereas low-quality definitions are not specific enough to help.

Although it may be easy to select a problem behavior, clearly defining that behavior so that it can be accurately identified by several different individuals working with a student is more difficult. For example, the phrase *disruptive behavior* may conjure up images of annoying verbal behaviors (e.g., burping, yelling, humming) for one of us, whereas someone else may picture a child running around the classroom. Thus, in addition to defining a behavior by placing it into

TABLE 3.3

High- and Low-Quality Problem Definitions

High-Quality Definitions	Low-Quality Definitions
Ramona engages in self-injurious behavior, including hitting and banging her head when frustrated.	Ramona beats herself up.
John complies with his mother's request to pick up his clothes only when provided with at least four reminders.	John never listens to his mother.
Sam displays low on-task behavior (looking around, head on desk) during independent work time.	Sam doesn't pay attention in class.
Nicole kicks peers when she is asked to share on the playground.	Nicole is an aggressive child.
Tracy completes and turns in one out of three homework assignments.	Tracy doesn't do her homework.

a broad category, it is helpful to provide an explanation of that category or examples of behavior in that category to ensure that everyone is clear about what the target behavior is and is not. Table 3.4 provides operational definitions of some common referral complaints. Further operational definitions relevant to school settings can be found in various observational coding systems, such as the State-Event Classroom Observation System (SECOS; Saudargas, 1997), the Behavioral Observation of Students in Schools (BOSS; Shapiro, 1996a), and the Behavioral Objective Sequence (BOS; Braaten, 1998).

After selected target behaviors are operationally defined, the FBA process requires that baseline levels (measures of the current level of behavior) be established. At this point, we advise that some discussion center on the potential intervention monitoring techniques and the preliminary goals for behavior change. As we already stated, replacement behaviors and positively stated intervention goals will be developed later. However, these considerations are important at this stage because the FBA process requires that baseline measures of target behavior, intervention monitoring, and goals all be assessed with consistent techniques. For instance, direct observational information may indicate that John is off-task in math class 50 percent of the time. But if resources are not available to monitor the outcomes of the ensuing intervention with direct observation, then perhaps a less accurate but more feasible data collection method (e.g., daily teacher ratings of on-task behavior during math) might be used to reestablish baseline levels (e.g., a mean teacher rating of 2 out of 5 on-task behaviors at baseline), develop goals (student will earn teacher ratings of 4 or higher for on-task behavior

TABLE 3.4

Operational Definitions of Common Problem Behaviors

Broad Behavior Category	Possible Operational Definitions
Noncompliant behavior	Student fails to follow individual or group request by adult within five seconds.
Disruptive behavior	Student interferes with instruction by being out of seat, calling out, or making other disruptive noises.
Negative peer interaction	Student engages in potentially inflammatory interactions with classmates by threatening, gesturing, being verbally disruptive, or bothering or harassing peers.
Off-task activity	Student is not oriented toward the teacher or actively engaged in instructional activities.
Physical aggression	Student hits, kicks, pinches, pushes, or hurts others.

in math class by October 14), and then monitor the intervention over time. Further, baseline levels of easily identified replacement behaviors might also be collected because intervention goals are often written in positive terms. For example, baseline rates of positive social interaction, compliance, and work completion might also be included to inform intervention design and evaluation. Therefore, wise practitioners will save time and energy by ensuring that problem identification statements include baseline levels that are consistent with feasible intervention goals and monitoring techniques.

Measure Target Behaviors

After a target behavior has been operationalized, it is time to determine how that behavior will be measured, bearing in mind the previous statement that the intervention monitoring technique and the statement of the goal need to employ the same measure, as described in the preceding paragraph. Baseline data are important because the information serves as the reference point to assess progress during the intervention. Generally, no fewer than three baseline points are collected in order to ensure that estimates of the problem behavior are relatively accurate. If only one estimate is collected, it is not possible to know for sure if it reflects the true behavior or if perhaps some other factor interfered with the behavior at that time. Thus collecting data at more than one point and making sure that those points are fairly consistent (not highly variable) make it easier to evaluate change in behavior later on.

Three main dimensions of behavior are often referenced: frequency, duration, and intensity. *Frequency* refers to the number of times the behavior occurs in the specified period (e.g., number of call-outs per hour), whereas *duration* refers to the length of time over which the behavior occurs (e.g., minutes of each temper tantrum). In contrast, *inten-*

sity provides a more general measure of the disruptive or dangerous nature of the behavior. For example, the behavior might be rated high intensity if the safety of the student or others is in question, whereas a behavior that is disruptive to the class might be rated medium intensity. A low-intensity rating might be given to noncompliant behaviors that are not particularly disruptive or dangerous.

Chapter 5 discusses data collection in detail and describes specific procedures, but a few words about the selection of techniques are warranted here because the type of baseline data collected or needed will vary depending on the situation. The gold standard of data collection is usually direct observation. However, the constraints of applied settings must be acknowledged, particularly as related to school resources. These constraints usually limit the number of cases in which labor-intensive data collection procedures such as direct observation can be used. We suggest that the method for collecting baseline information be tied to the need for accuracy in the hypothesis about the behavior. The quality of various methods differs widely, but all can be appropriate in different situations. A higher quality method would be selected for truly high-stakes cases, when it is important to generate a more accurate hypothesis (reason) for the behavior. Thus, for behaviors involving serious disruption or potential harm to the student or others, or when placement of a student in a more restrictive setting is being considered, it may be wise to invest in a higher quality data collection technique. For behaviors considered mildly annoying rather than seriously disruptive, a less rigorous technique, like self-monitoring or a teacher's completion of a rating scale, would likely suffice.

The quality of a data collection technique is usually based on its directness. One standard for determining directness is whether the collected information is removed in time and place from the actual occurrence of the behavior (Cone, 1978). Interviews and rating scales are considered indirect because the information is collected from another person, who must rely on recollections about the behavior; in contrast, in direct observation, information is recorded about an event as it actually occurs. The same situation exists for assessment of academic problems: Most norm-referenced standardized tests provide valuable information but do not provide direct, repeated information about specific academic performance in the classroom. More direct academic measures include curriculum-based assessment procedures or classroom assessments such as weekly quizzes.

Once the data collection procedure has been chosen, it is implemented in order to determine the baseline level of behavior. The problem identification stage is completed when up to two target behaviors have been selected, defined, and measured. Table 3.5 gives examples of problem identification statements incorporating baseline levels.

The following case example illustrates the FBA process so far:

> *Steve is referred for physical altercations with peers in the classroom. His teacher states that these altercations are often preceded by apparent frustration with independent seatwork. Steve becomes frustrated, then goes off-task and gets out of his seat to wander around the room. During these times, he*

TABLE 3.5

Problem Identification Statements

1. John completes independent worksheets involving single-digit multiplication problems with an average of 50 percent accuracy.

2. During whole-group instruction, Keisha calls out without raising her hand an average of eight times per 45-minute period.

3. When playing tag on the playground, Petey is observed pushing peers to the ground an average of two times per half-hour recess.

4. Ramona tantrums (refuses adult requests, drops to the floor, yells, and kicks at others) an average of two times per week with high intensity and an average duration of nine minutes.

is most likely to have a physical or near-physical altercation with another student. The teacher has identified a suspected behavior chain for Steve: leaving his seat during independent work time often predicts physical altercations with other students. As a result, both of these behaviors are selected for consideration during the problem identification stage. Further, because the educational consultant involved in this case has her eye toward intervention design, she positively states one of the behavioral targets. She therefore provides these definitions of Steve's target behaviors: altercations with other students *(hitting, harassing, or posturing to hurt others)* and completing work in his desk area *(the extent to which Steve completes assigned tasks in his area and appropriately requests assistance when required). These behaviors are measured by directly documenting each altercation occurance and by teacher ratings of work completion on a scale of one to five made after each academic period. During the intervention development stage, goals will be set to decrease Steve's altercations with other students but also to increase teacher ratings of his completing work at his desk and appropriately requesting assistance.*

Putting It All Together

The problem identification stage begins with a review of relevant background information about the student and situation, gathered from multiple sources, to gain an understanding of the problems involved. Specifically, the referral source and other participants in the process generate potential targets for intervention, then prioritize them to narrow the list to one or two target behaviors. The selected behaviors are then operationally defined and measured at baseline with a technique also feasible for intervention monitoring. The problem identification stage concludes when a problem identification statement is developed for each target behavior, including an operational definition and a current baseline level. In essence, the problem identification stage is final when the following questions have been addressed:

1. Has a list of problem behaviors been identified and prioritized?

2. Have one or two of those behaviors been selected as targets?

3. Have replacement behaviors, intervention goals, and precursor behaviors been considered when selecting targets?

4. Are those target behaviors defined in a measurable and observable format?

5. Has a baseline data collection strategy been selected and conducted?

6. Has a problem identification statement, including the operational definition and baseline level of the problem, been written?

CHAPTER 4

Problem Investigation and Analysis

The school psychologist has conducted three classroom observations of Joey, using a narrative ABC format. Meanwhile, the teacher has used a daily behavior report card to assess teacher ratings of Joey's behavior and completed a daily behavior log to document each of Joey's tantrums. The school psychologist observed several instances of noncompliance during transitions when the teacher issued a group directive (e.g., "Class, please take out your books and turn to page 11") and within two to three seconds began prompting individual students who were not following directions. At times, Joey did not comply after his individual prompt; instead, he crossed his arms over his chest and sank down in his chair. When pressed again, he would sink even lower in his chair. In addition to teacher redirection, then, noncompliance also appeared to be associated with task transitions during group instruction. Consequences observed included reprimands, having one's name written on the board, and loss of incentive time. Although no tantrums were observed, teacher log information indicated that noncompliance often preceded tantrums and that they occurred most often during language arts time. Further investigation revealed that Joey has academic delays, particularly in the areas of reading and writing. Thus Joey's noncompliant and tantrum behaviors appear to be escape-related: to escape the task, demand, or setting. Joey's strengths include a desire to assist others; he does well when asked to complete special jobs in school, and at home he consistently completes a small list of daily chores for his aunt.

The problem investigation and analysis stage is the heart of the FBA process. This is when the true detective work begins. One major goal of this stage of the process is to identify the conditions that predict, support, or influence the occurrence of problem behavior in order to inform the development of the intervention plan. In addition, this analysis requires identifying student strengths and motivators, as well as selecting replacement behaviors to teach and promote during the ensuing intervention plan. Again, the Functional Behavioral Assessment Worksheet, in Appendix A, reflects the overall process. Here we discuss important assessment information to help readers complete the worksheet, which in turn will inform intervention design. Appendix B provides charts detailing considerations in analyzing behavior problems during assessment and intervention.

In brief, problem analysis first requires consideration of relevant background information as it relates to well-defined target behaviors (as explained in chapters 2 and 3). Next, a more in-depth investigation of factors that influence the occurrence of problem behavior begins. Conditions that predict the behavior are investigated, including (a) distant predictors (events removed in time or space that increase the likelihood

TABLE 4.1

Stage 2: Problem Investigation and Analysis

Stage 1: Problem Identification

Stage 2: Problem Investigation and Analysis
- Identify conditions that predict the behavior.
- Identify skill deficits and communicative intent.
- Develop a functional theory (hypothesis) about why the behavior occurs.
- Identify strengths, interests, and potential replacement behaviors.

Stage 3: Intervention Plan Development and Implementation

Stage 4: Intervention Plan Evaluation

of problematic behavior), (b) more immediate antecedent variables that appear to trigger or directly predict behavior, (c) problematic settings and activities, and (d) consequences that typically occur subsequent to the behavior.

During the problem investigation and analysis stage, it is also important to make sure that the student has the academic, behavioral, and communicative skills to function adequately in the classroom. All of this information is then summarized into a testable functional theory, or hypothesis. The last, and often most important, step in this stage of the process is to identify the student's strengths, interests, and potential motivators, as well as to confirm replacement behaviors that will better serve the student's interests. Table 4.1 summarizes the components of the investigation and analysis stage. The remainder of the chapter explains this stage in greater detail.

Identify Conditions That Predict the Behavior

During problem analysis and investigation, a thorough exploration is conducted for each target behavior selected during problem identification. The goal is to identify conditions that predict or influence the selected target behavior. First, background information is used to identify *distant predictors* that may precede or predict the behavior. These events do not happen at the same time or in the same place as the problem behavior, but they influence its occurrence. Examples include poor sleep, harassment prior to school, issues relating to parental divorce, and many of the individual and contextual factors reviewed in chapter 2. O'Neill et al. (1997) have listed some areas to assess when looking for distant predictors:

Medications currently prescribed

Physical difficulties

Sleep difficulties

Nutritional difficulties

Daily schedule

Contributing factors from home and community

Critical or traumatic events that have recently occurred

Distant predictors cover a broad spectrum of variables; they may be school-based, home-based, physiological, and so on. Sorting the conditions that predict challenging behavior into setting events, establishing operations, or identifying classroom antecedents can be confusing to those without a background in applied behavioral analysis. For our purposes, we are more interested in having school-based professionals identify salient conditions that predict behavior than having them correctly classify them into the appropriate categories. For this reason, we have simplified the assessment process by listing predictive conditions on the FBA Worksheet as *distant predictors* (physiological factors or factors removed in time and setting from the behavior) and school-based *precursor behaviors*, which typically occur at the beginning of identified *behavior chains*. This portion of the worksheet is shown in Figure 4.1.

Behavior chains are the smaller behaviors that link to the larger episodes. Direct observation or teacher interviews can identify these smaller, precursor behaviors. Because precursor behaviors are exhibited prior to larger, more intense episodes, it is important to identify precursor behaviors to devise interventions to prevent more disruptive and unsafe behaviors. Precursors may include fairly passive behaviors, like facial grimacing, staring, or social withdrawal (e.g., a student's pulling a hood down over his head), or active behaviors, including motoric excess (e.g., leg bouncing, pencil tapping), wandering around the classroom, or loud verbalizations. These behaviors are then listed on the FBA Worksheet. They will become important considerations later, during the intervention design process.

After considering distant predictors and precursor behaviors, the assessment moves to the conditions that immediately surround the identified behavior, essentially telling us what happens before, during, and after the behavior occurs. Important areas to assess include time of day, physical setting, people, and activities that appear to trigger or predict problem behavior (O'Neill et al., 1997). In schools, typical antecedents or triggers include transitions (in task or setting), teacher redirection, and interruptions in routine (ranging from simple schedule changes to the arrival of a substitute teacher). Important setting and activity-related variables in the school often include a loud, crowded cafeteria, academic downtime in the classroom, and specific academic tasks (e.g., oral reading, independent seatwork). Further, as suggested in chapter 2, classroom variables such as task length and difficulty, instructional pace, and clarity of behavioral expectations may increase the expression of challenging behavior. Reviewing the student's daily schedule with the teacher may help to identify a number of *tasks*, *activities*, *settings*, *times*, and even *people* predicting the occurrence or nonoccurrence of problem behavior. Once these problematic issues are identified, they can be investigated in more depth. Figure 4.2 shows the portion of the FBA Worksheet devoted to these antecedents.

FIGURE 4.1

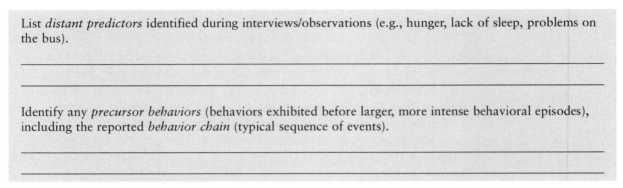

FBA Worksheet: Distant Predictors and Precursor Behaviors

List *distant predictors* identified during interviews/observations (e.g., hunger, lack of sleep, problems on the bus).

_____

_____

Identify any *precursor behaviors* (behaviors exhibited before larger, more intense behavioral episodes), including the reported *behavior chain* (typical sequence of events).

_____

_____

A variety of techniques may be used to conduct this more in-depth investigation and documentation of problem behavior. The data collection technique to use depends on the nature of the identified behavior. For example, frequently occurring behavior might be analyzed with a direct observation tool, such as a narrative procedure, in order to document the occurrence of negative behavior as well as antecedents, consequences, and setting variables. In contrast, infrequent but intense tantrum behaviors might most feasibly be documented with a behavior log and scatterplot procedure. Chapter 5 discusses the procedures involved in data collection more thoroughly.

Consequences that might support negative school behavior include teacher reprimand or redirection, removal of incentive, time-out, office referral, and suspension. The goal at this point is simply to document the consequences that occur following the problem behavior. For example, a student calling out in the classroom might be given three warnings and then asked to complete a 10-minute time-out in another teacher's classroom. All of this information will be used later in the process to develop a functional theory, or hypothesis, which, among other things, will stipulate how these identified consequences maintain or support the problematic behavior.

Because each of the general triggers/antecedents, settings and activities, and consequences identified in this portion of the assessment will require later accommodation through the individualized intervention, it is important for practitioners to limit their selection of these variables to those that are most predictive or have the greatest influence on the expression of the selected target behavior or behaviors. (The narrative ABC or scatterplot and behavior log procedures are particularly well suited for identifying or validating these variables.)

Identify Skill Deficits and Communicative Intent

Sometimes a student's negative behavior is related to lack of skill, either academic or behavioral, or it serves as a mode of communication. Therefore, another part of problem investigation is assessing for the presence of behavioral or academic skill deficits and for communicative intent. For example, a primary grade student lacking

FIGURE 4.2

FBA Worksheet: Immediate Antecedents and Consequences

IMMEDIATE ANTECEDENTS AND CONSEQUENCES

From the following list, select the conditions that appear to predict and support each problem behavior. Include the triggers, problematic settings and activities, and consequences.

Triggers/antecedents	Problematic settings/activities	Consequences
❑ Lack of social attention	❑ Independent seatwork	❑ Behavior ignored
❑ Demand/request	❑ Group instruction	❑ Reprimand/warning
❑ Difficult task	❑ Crowded setting	❑ Time-out
❑ Transition (task/setting)	❑ Unstructured activity	❑ Loss of incentives
❑ Specific time of day	❑ Unstructured setting	❑ Sent to office
❑ Interruption in routine	❑ Academic downtime	❑ Home communication
❑ Negative social interaction	❑ Special subjects	❑ In-school suspension
❑ Consequences imposed	❑ Specific task/subject	❑ Out-of-school suspension
❑ Specific people *(List)*	*(List)* _____	❑ Restraint
_____	❑ Other _____	❑ Other _____
_____	❑ Other _____	❑ Other _____

basic skills in written expression may become noncompliant and disruptive when asked to complete an independent writing assignment. In this scenario, a critical part of an intervention may be to offer the student additional instruction and increased support to complete writing tasks—that is, to teach the necessary skills.

The referred child's behavioral, academic, and communication skills are considered in the school context as they relate to the occurrence of the target behavior or behaviors. The evaluator reviews the information collected (e.g., interviews, observations, other assessment results, such as of speech and language) and decides whether the student appears to have the necessary skills to function productively in the current setting. If not, then one component of the intervention will need to focus on skill development—either increasing positive adaptive behaviors, academic skills, and supports or developing functional communication skills. Figure 4.3 shows the portion of the worksheet devoted to instructional and communicative needs.

Academic Skills

A student's academic skills are usually the first area of focus during skill assessment because a mismatch between skill level and the curriculum can make challenging behavior especially difficult to diminish. In other words, an instructional match between the student's current skills and the curriculum is important. Information from sources such as teacher, parent, and student interviews; report cards; work samples; and stan-

FIGURE 4.3

FBA Worksheet: Relationship of Problem Behavior to Skill Deficits and Communication

INSTRUCTIONAL AND COMMUNICATIVE NEEDS

Is the student's problem behavior believed to be related to skill deficit or communication needs? *(Check any that apply.)*

Skill deficits		Communication needs
Academic deficit	*Behavioral deficit*	*Communicative intent*
❑ Work is too hard	❑ Lacks the expected behavior	❑ To request assistance
❑ Not enough practice	❑ Needs practice/modeling	❑ To request a break
❑ Not enough help	❑ Requires more structure	❑ To indicate a need
❑ Skill not generalized	❑ Can't apply skill across settings	❑ To indicate frustration
❑ Other _____	❑ Other _____	❑ Other _____

dardized tests will help the evaluator identify areas of academic concern. A more complete analysis of the student's current instructional level and specific difficulties with subject areas of concern can then be conducted. Curriculum-based assessment is particularly well-suited for this purpose because these procedures provide a relatively quick and direct assessment of the student's skills in the actual curriculum (see Gravois & Gickling, 2002; Shapiro, 1996a, 1996b). Other frequent classroom-based performance assessments, such as weekly quizzes and homework grades, may also help determine patterns of strength and weakness.

As chapter 2 indicated, the instructional hierarchy has been promoted as an effective model for the assessment of academic functioning and the identification of appropriate intervention (Daly, Witt, Martens, & Dool, 1997; see Figure 2.2). Using the instructional hierarchy, the assessment of academic skills starts with ensuring effective instruction and instructional match and then moves on to a thorough assessment of the student's stage in the learning process (i.e., accuracy, fluency, and generalization). If a mismatch between skill level and instruction is revealed, then specific and more appropriate modifications to instructional strategies are identified. Chapter 8 discusses specific interventions for academic skill deficits, especially at the initial stages in the learning process.

Behavioral Skills

In a similar fashion, the student may lack the skills to meet behavioral expectations or, in other words, have a behavioral skill deficit. For example, the student may need to be taught how to take turns, how to manage anger, how to resolve conflict, or how to ask for help in the classroom. During this stage of the assessment, the evaluator looks for the presence of required behavioral skills. The primary question here is "Does the student ever, in any setting, display the required skills?" If the student has the skills (e.g., hand raising, active listening, hallway transitioning skills), then the intervention will focus on promoting these behaviors in the desired setting. Behavioral skill instruction is called for when the child lacks the skills—as opposed to the motivation—to perform the desired behavior, and skill instruction must be part of the intervention plan. (Chapter 8 also considers interventions that address behavioral skill deficits.)

Communication Skills

In addition to assessing for the presence of academic and behavioral skill deficits, the evaluator should assess communicative intent as related to the target behavior. Although students in general may misbehave in order to communicate displeasure, frustration with a task, or a desire to engage in a preferred activity, these students are capable of verbally communicating their needs and are generally easy to redirect. The communicative intent of a student exhibiting challenging behavior, however, may be different in populations of children with difficulties in verbal expression—for example, young children and those with speech delays, pervasive developmental disorders, or cognitive delays. These children are more likely to communicate a greater variety of their needs through negative behavior. If it appears that the child does not have the skills to communicate basic needs effectively, then a relevant form of communication training may be needed. For example, the first author consulted on the case of a fourth grader with autism referred because of physically aggressive behaviors toward staff. After observations of the student and interviews with his educational team, it was determined that the aggressive behavior served to communicate academic frustration and a desire to stop a given task. Therefore, the designed intervention involved teaching and reinforcing an alternate way to communicate frustration and to request a break (the student would point to a break symbol on a picture board at his desk).

Develop a Functional Theory

After assessing for the presence of skill deficits and communicative intent, the evaluator next considers consequences that might be supporting the behavior. For instance, a child having a tantrum in the candy aisle of the local grocery store may learn that her behavior can result in a reward: If she receives candy to quiet her, the lesson she quickly learns is that tantrum behavior results in her getting the desired item.

Understanding the Functions of Behavior

In the school setting, it has been suggested that the function of most negative classroom behavior is to gain attention (teacher attention, peer attention) or to escape from academic tasks and activities (Vollmer & Northrup, 1996). Frequently, negative behavior serves to get the child something desired (positive reinforcement) or allows the child to escape from something perceived as aversive (negative reinforcement). Behavior that is positively reinforced results in an increase in attention (e.g., teacher, peer) or access to a preferred activity, person, area, or item (as in the example of the child's demand for candy). Alternatively, some students misbehave in order to escape nonpreferred tasks, activities, or areas (i.e., negative reinforcement). An example is the student who would rather be sent to the office for disruptive behavior than persist with boring and difficult class work. Similarly, students with heightened sensory awareness, such as some autistic children, may seek to escape loud or "busy" settings that provide overwhelming sensory input. The function of negative behavior, then, is to get something perceived as desirable (attention, candy, stimulation) or to get away from something perceived as aversive (such as seatwork, loud settings). In addition, a behavior may be automatically reinforced through the sensory or perceptual stimulation the individual experiences while engaging in it (e.g., humming, flapping, spinning). Most often, behaviors supported by automatic reinforcement are observed in special populations of multiply disabled or cognitively delayed individuals, and are identified by their repetitive and stereotypic nature.

Assessing the Functions of Behavior

Methods used to assess the function of behavior are usually divided into two categories: descriptive assessment and functional analysis (sometimes known as experimental analysis). Although each method can be useful in certain situations, the two should not be considered parallel forms of the same test (Noell, VanDerHeyden, Gatti, & Whitmarsh, 2001). That is, although both methods may be useful in identifying conditions that influence behavior, they vary in complexity, accuracy, and expertise required for implementation.

For less serious or complex behaviors (e.g., calling out during math class), *descriptive assessment* may be sufficient. Descriptive assessment refers to the collection and examination of baseline data, after which hypotheses about the function of behavior are generated. Thus the hypotheses developed through descriptive assessments are not directly tested. Data collection techniques include observation, interviews, and rating scales. As reviewed in chapter 5, these techniques also vary in the accuracy and specificity of the information obtained. Although descriptive assessments may not identify hypotheses as precisely as do functional analyses, they can be helpful in identifying conditions that influence behavior, and this identification may suffice for certain purposes. In the public school setting, for example, interviewing the parent and teacher or teachers and asking the question "Does the behavior result in the student's gaining teacher or peer attention or escaping certain academic tasks?" may result in a functional theory that is adequate to inform intervention design.

In more complex or high-stakes cases (e.g., in the case of a child who exhibits self-injurious behavior or is at risk of removal from the classroom), *functional analysis* may be necessary in order to reach a more accurate hypothesis about the behavior. In functional analysis, variables are systematically manipulated in order to test directly the impact of each one on the behavior (Vollmer & Northrup, 1996). For

TABLE 4.2

Pros and Cons of Assessment Methods

Experimental Assessment

—*Functional analysis, brief experimental analysis, analogue assessment*

Pros: Can identify conditions influencing behavior

Most precise hypothesis generated

Cons: Practical challenges to implementation in applied setting

Potential disruption to class routine

Potential increase in problem behavior in some conditions

Descriptive Assessment

—*Direct observation, rating scales, interviews*

Pros: Can identify conditions influencing behavior

Limited disruption to class routine

Cons: Less conclusive hypothesis generated

Decreasing strength of hypothesis regarding function

example, if it is suggested that a problem behavior such as self-injurious behavior (SIB) is related to teacher attention, then this hypothesis could be tested by using functional analysis. In this scenario, direct observation may be used to collect rates of SIB across two conditions: (a) the teacher attends to the student each time SIB occurs (high-attention condition) and (b) the teacher ignores all SIB behavior and attends to the child only during SIB-free intervals (low-attention condition). If the attention hypothesis is correct, then SIB rates should be consistently higher in the first condition. These procedures require that the student be exposed to specified and well-controlled conditions (i.e., high attention/low attention) in order to test the functional hypothesis. In addition, data collection during functional analysis involves the use of direct observation techniques, which are generally more time-consuming than indirect methods. For a more detailed discussion of functional analysis procedures, see O'Neill et al. (1997). Table 4.2 (summarized from Noell et al., 2001) lists some pros and cons of experimental and descriptive assessment.

Once the assessment has been accomplished, the suspected function of the student's behavior should be listed on the FBA Worksheet (see Figure 4.4). As we have seen, through functional analysis, functional theories are tested in controlled conditions to identify a single, primary function for a given target behavior. However, practitioners using descriptive procedures are also advised to focus on one function for each target behavior. Selecting two or more functions for a target behavior will lead to confusion during the intervention design stage. Furthermore, inability to narrow down the list likely indicates a need for a more thorough analysis (e.g., a narrative ABC).

FIGURE 4.4

FBA Worksheet: Possible Functions of Identified Behaviors

FUNCTIONS OF BEHAVIOR

What function(s) do the identified behavior(s) seem to serve for the child?

To gain something:

Attention/control	Gain desired item, activity, area	Sensory/perceptual feedback
❏ Gain adult attention	❏ Gain access to a desired item	❏ Gain automatic sensory stimulation
❏ Gain peer attention	❏ Gain access to a desired activity	
❏ Get attention of a preferred adult	❏ Gain access to a desired area	❏ Gain perceptual reinforcement
	❏ Other _____	❏ Other _____
❏ Other _____		

To escape or avoid something:

❏ Avoid a demand or request	❏ Avoid a person	❏ Other _____
❏ Avoid an activity/task (if known)	❏ Escape the school	❏ Other _____

In practice, some typical problem behaviors may appear to have more than one maintaining consequence or function. For instance, consequences for disruptive classroom behavior may include teacher attention in addition to removal from the classroom. In a descriptive assessment, clarifying questions can be used to hypothesize one primary function. Questions might include the following: "Where does the student go when asked to leave the room?" "Does she appear upset when asked to leave?" "How many warnings is she given prior to removal?" and "Does she appear to crave teacher or peer attention?" In this scenario, the teacher's answers to clarifying questions may suggest that the primary function of the behavior is escape because the student appears to enjoy being removed from the classroom and resting in the in-school suspension room. In high-stakes cases, when resources permit, or when clarifying questions do not assist in identifying one behavioral function, then observational procedures are strongly advised.

At this point in the analysis, the following activities have been completed: (a) target behavior or behaviors have been defined; (b) baseline measures have been collected; (c) antecedents (distant, precursor, and immediate behaviors), concurrent/setting variables, and consequences have been identified; (d) existing skill deficits and communicative intent have been assessed; and (e) the primary functions of the behaviors have been hypothesized. This information is now organized and summarized into a statement of the functional theory. The *functional theory*, or hypothesis, is a statement including information collected and organized in a way that is easily tested and presented to the referring teacher or parent. Figure 4.5 shows the portion of the FBA Worksheet for recording that statement.

FIGURE 4.5

FBA Worksheet: Functional Theory Statement

FUNCTIONAL THEORY STATEMENT

State hypothesis about behavior in the following form:

When _____ occur(s) in the context of _____ ,
    (triggers/antecedents)   *(settings/activities)*
the student displays _____ in order to _____ ,
                    (target behavior[s])   *(perceived function)*
and these target behavior(s) may be related to _____ .
                                        (skill deficit/communicative intent, when present)

A sample functional theory statement is as follows:

> When a lack of attention or a transition *(triggers/antecedents)* occurs in the context of large-group instruction *(settings, activities)*, the student displays loud, disruptive, and calling-out behaviors *(target behaviors)* in order to gain attention *(perceived function)*.

Similarly, when a skill deficit or communicative deficit is suspected, a statement reflecting those deficits should be incorporated into the functional theory, adjacent to the function. The following example, adapted from a publication on FBA by the New York State Education Department (1998), illustrates:

> When an independent or oral reading task *(triggers/antecedents)* occurs in the context of group instruction *(settings, activities)*, the student displays off-task and disruptive behavior *(target behaviors)* in order to escape the task *(perceived function)*, and these target behaviors may be related to delayed reading skills *(skill deficit, communicative intent)*.

Identify Replacement Behaviors, Problem-Free Times, and Potential Motivators

Although the problem analysis process focuses primarily on the student's negative behavior, this last step in the process, in contrast, identifies (a) what positive behaviors the student exhibits that potentially could replace the problem behavior yet serve the same function, (b) under which circumstances target behavior does not occur, and (c) what incentives and motivators might increase the occurrence of positive behavior. The idea here is that the ensuing intervention will leverage the student's strengths to promote a positive replacement behavior with preferred incentives or motivators that may also be functionally relevant. Figure 4.6 shows the portion of the FBA Worksheet devoted to this information.

Understanding the student's strengths, interests, and preferences is important in developing an individualized intervention. Teacher, parent, and student interviews are a

FIGURE 4.6

FBA Worksheet:
Replacement Behaviors, Problem-Free Times, and Potential Motivators

REPLACEMENT BEHAVIORS, PROBLEM-FREE TIMES, AND POTENTIAL MOTIVATORS

Replacement behaviors: What competing adaptive behavior could replace each target behavior and still serve the same function for the student?

_____

_____

When, where, and with whom is the target behavior typically *not* displayed?

_____

_____

List some some potential incentives or motivators for the student.

_____

_____

good way to begin to accomplish this goal. The following are examples of questions that might be asked during these interviews:

> What academic, vocational, or social strengths does the student possess?

> Are there settings, activities, and persons with whom the negative behavior is typically *not* displayed?

> Are there roles, responsibilities, tasks, or incentives that would motivate the student to display more positive behavior?

As noted previously, a replacement behavior is one that is more socially desirable than the target behavior yet serves the same function for the student. For example, using a three-minute hall pass may be an acceptable replacement for disruptive classroom behavior and may serve the equivalent function of giving the student a break from academic tasks. As suggested in chapter 3, replacement behaviors should begin to be considered during the problem identification stage. At that point, the evaluator should consider the target behavior and look for easily identified replacement behaviors. When the challenging behavior is fairly straightforward—a student's getting out of his seat or calling out without raising his hand, for example—identifying replacement behaviors may be simple (e.g., work in seat, raise hand). But when the behavior is more complex (e.g., tantrums) or is related to prominent predictive conditions (e.g., AD/HD), replacement behaviors are often less clear. In these cases, replacement behaviors are often identified only after the problem analysis stage, when there is a better understanding of the target behavior, predictive conditions, and behavioral function. Based on this model, assessment information derived from the problem investigation and analysis process can be linked directly to the behavior intervention plan. Chapter 6 discusses how to diagram target and replacement behaviors through a competing pathways model.

The following case example briefly illustrates an analysis of one student's classroom behavior. (Chapter 6 continues with this case.)

Jason, a third grader, loves playing the part of class clown. He exhibits calling-out behavior (defined as verbal comments other students can hear without first raising his hand and being called on by the teacher) that is disrupting instruction in the classroom. An interview with the teacher suggests that Jason's behavior is especially prevalent during direct, whole-class instruction (e.g., during math, social studies, and science). The teacher, using a golf-stroke counter, conducts her own frequency counts of Jason's call-outs. Over the course of three such assessments, she determines that, on average, Jason makes eight call-outs per 45-minute instructional period. It is then hypothesized that when direct instruction occurs in the context of large-group or classwide settings, Jason displays calling-out behavior in order to gain peer and teacher attention. The teacher often ignores Jason's call-outs or writes his name on the board and uses a check system (three checks, and you're out), which she uses with the entire class. Additional interview information indicates that Jason knows the expected hand-raising behavior, likes to read, and is quite social. Initial ideas for intervention include altering the consequences for his call-outs, increasing attention for alternative behavior (hand raising), and capitalizing on Jason's social and academic strengths.

Putting It All Together

After problem identification, the problem investigation and analysis stage begins with an exploration of the conditions that influence the target behavior or behaviors. These conditions include distant predictors and precursor behaviors (especially as they occur in behavior chains), immediate antecedents or triggers that usually precede the behavior (including setting and activities), and the consequences that usually follow. Next, existing academic or behavioral skill and communicative needs are assessed. The focus then shifts to hypothesizing the function of the target behavior. The problem analysis process is complete when the functional theory has been developed and a list of the student's strengths, likely incentives, and potential replacement behaviors has been generated. In chapter 6, we explain how this assessment information is used to select, design, and implement an individualized intervention plan.

CHAPTER 5

Assessment, Monitoring, and Evaluation Strategies

The target behaviors selected for Joey's intervention are noncompliance and tantrums. As described previously, during the problem identification stage baseline measures were collected, using a daily behavior report card (DBRC) to document compliance (average rating of 1.3 out of 5) and a behavior log to document tantrums (average of three per week, 12-minute duration, high intensity). The educators working with Joey decide that it would be feasible to continue to monitor compliance with a DBRC completed by the teacher twice a day, prior to lunch and prior to dismissal. They also decide that the behavior log is a good way to document tantrums, given their weekly frequency. After the group selects monitoring techniques, they develop goals to inform intervention design. These goals are to do the following within two weeks: (a) decrease the frequency of tantrums to no more than one per week, with a duration no greater than 6 minutes and intensity reduced to medium (no aggression toward staff or students), and (b) increase average daily compliance ratings on the DBRC to 3 (out of 5) or higher. Previous use of the monitoring techniques provides a baseline measure of each target behavior, helps establish initial goals for intervention, and will provide a way to track progress toward each goal.

Collecting objective assessment information and consistently monitoring behavior over time can be a challenge in the school setting. Absences, snow days, vacations, mandated assessments, and a variety of other unforeseen obstacles arise that may interfere with everyone's best intentions. Nevertheless, this information is crucial to the intervention process. In this chapter, we emphasize the importance of selecting the most efficient yet effective procedure to do the job. We discuss how behavior intervention and monitoring plans should outline a feasible technique for measuring each target behavior and include the baseline-level information, intervention goals, and plans for evaluating student progress toward the established goals. A wide range of procedures may be used to monitor and evaluate student progress, including direct observation, interviews, and rating scales. Which specific procedures to use depends on the desired type of information, the resources available to collect the information, and the degree of accuracy required. The narrative ABC and the behavior log and scatterplot procedures are examples of behavioral assessment techniques that can document the influence of environmental and school-based variables (activity, time of day, etc.) on student behavior. After reviewing the reasons for measuring behavior and the selection of a monitoring technique, we conclude the chapter with an overview of specific techniques. The following reproducible forms, one for each technique described, are provided at the end of the chapter:

Reasons for Measuring Behavior

Soon after the target behavior is operationalized, it is time to determine how that behavior will be measured during both the analysis and intervention phases of the process. Reasons to measure behavior are as follows:

1. To provide preintervention information about behavior (an objective assessment of conditions that influence behavior and baseline levels of the behavior)

2. To set ambitious yet realistic goals for the student

3. To evaluate short- and long-term progress toward goals

The focus of the problem investigation and analysis stage, described in chapter 4, is on identifying predictive conditions. After the conditions that influence the expression of the target behavior have been established, a consistent method must be used to collect baseline information, set goals for the student, and monitor and evaluate student progress.

For instance, three ABC observations used to measure the calling-out behavior of a student may suggest that relevant predictive conditions include seat placement at the back of the room and slow transitions between academic tasks, and that peer attention appears to be a powerful maintaining consequence for the behavior. The ABC may also indicate that the student calls out an average of 5 times per 20-minute observation (a rate of 15 times per hour). This information informs the design of the intervention (in this case, changing seat placement and structuring transitions). The baseline levels documented (15 call-outs per hour) may be used as a benchmark to set intervention goals and to evaluate student progress.

As we saw in earlier chapters, behavioral measurement techniques are generally used to identify conditions that predict or maintain challenging behaviors, especially in high-stakes cases or when other information is unclear or contradictory. Again, it is important that these techniques be used to identify maintaining and predictive conditions as well as to establish an accurate estimate of the current baseline level of behavior.

We have stated many times that it is important to use the same techniques for baseline assessment and for monitoring. It is also important to note that the shift from assessment to monitoring often involves turning the collection of data over to a different staff member. In these cases, we strongly advise training the new rater and then checking that person's reliability, or consistency with the other rater's findings. This is especially important if an independent observer, such as the school psychologist, conducts ABC observations for assessment and baseline information and then turns the intervention monitoring over to the teacher or another staff member. In this scenario, the independent observer should review the problem definition, provide training, review the monitoring procedures and forms, and complete two to three observations while the new observer is also documenting behavior. At the end of the observation period, results can be compared, and discrepancies can be addressed through clarification or retraining.

One strategy in conducting ABC observations of discrete behaviors consists of having the independent observer and teacher or staff member collect frequency data on the student's behavior during the same period of time. This procedure can be conducted until the teacher and observer collect consistent data and some stability in the baseline data emerges.

Generally, no fewer than three baseline points should be collected to ensure that estimates of the problem behavior represent actual behavior. If only one estimate is collected, evaluators will not be sure whether it reflects the true level of behavior or if some other factor interfered. In addition, making sure that those points are fairly consistent (i.e., stable) makes it easier later to evaluate change in behavior (see Figure 5.1). Variable baseline data generally require that more information be collected over a longer period of time, until the points become more stable.

After the baseline information is collected, it is time to set goals for intervention and design an intervention monitoring plan. A schedule for monitoring the behavior (e.g., daily, twice a week) should be developed based on the particular intervention. For example, even though an academic intervention may be implemented daily, it may be sufficient to monitor progress only twice a week because noticeable change is not likely to occur each day. In contrast, daily monitoring of aggressive playground behavior may be needed because of safety concerns or if the intervention plan ties daily behavior ratings to weekly incentives. Again, regardless of the monitoring schedule, the same data collected during baseline should be collected during intervention implementation in order to document change accurately. In addition, it may be useful to collect peer comparison data as a reference point for what is typical in a classroom. When selecting a peer (or several peers) for comparison, it is important to make sure the peer is the same gender as the target student, to account for developmental differences and differences in behavioral expression in girls and boys. The Monitoring Summary Sheet (Worksheet 5.7) may be useful for summarizing baseline information and information about the intervention.

FIGURE 5.1

Stable versus Variable Baseline Data

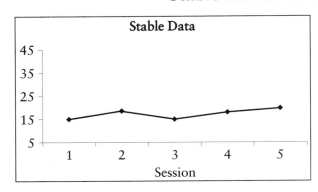

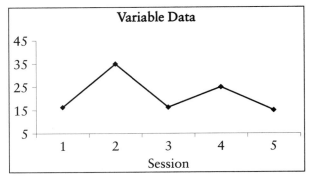

Last, the monitoring information collected will be used to evaluate intervention effectiveness. During evaluation, measures of the behavior prior to, during, and after intervention implementation are reviewed and compared with the goals for change. Plan evaluation allows evaluators to make informed decisions about whether to continue, modify, or terminate an intervention plan.

Selecting the Measurement and Monitoring Procedure

There are three key considerations when selecting a specific technique: (a) resource availability, (b) seriousness or intensity of the behavior, and (c) the match between the monitoring procedure and the behavior to be measured. Although some monitoring strategies have greater empirical support than others, these procedures usually require a greater allocation of resources (i.e., time, trained personnel) and therefore may need to be reserved for those cases that are more serious or intense (e.g., those involving unsafe or persistently disruptive behavior). Basically, the method chosen for collecting information should be tied to the needed confidence in generating and testing the hypothesis for the behavior. The gold standard of data collection is direct observation. This is because data are collected at the time and place in which the behavior actually occurs, with limited reliance on memory or perception. Direct observation can take many forms, such as counting the number of times a student swears, writing a narrative account of the behavior, and examining the occurrence of behavior during specified intervals of time.

Despite the strengths of direct observation, its potential strain on resources must be acknowledged. Significant training is needed for some direct observation techniques to be accurate, and they may require the presence of an external observer (a person other than the teacher). Furthermore, low-frequency behavior (e.g., fighting) may not be easily captured by an observer. Thus, although direct observation may offer high-quality information, other methods may be more feasible

TABLE 5.1

Methods of Behavioral Assessment and Monitoring

	Direct	*Indirect*
Technique:	Objective Direct observation, frequency count procedure	Subjective Interview, daily behavior report card
Example:	Counting the number of call-outs during math class	Rating a student's class participation on a scale of 1 to 10
Best used for:	High-stakes case	Low-stakes case

in situations where resources are scarce or the problem behavior is only mildly disruptive. Although we would argue for the collection of the best possible information, we also acknowledge the constraints of the applied setting and therefore discuss both direct and indirect monitoring techniques in this chapter.

The directness of different methods is illustrated in Table 5.1 (see Cone, 1978). As the figure shows, interviews and rating scales are considered indirect because the information is collected from another person who judges what the behavior looks like; in contrast, in direct observation the information about the event is recorded as it actually occurs.

Furthermore, not all techniques are equally capable of measuring all behaviors. Frequently occurring behaviors are better suited to direct observation than behaviors that occur only once or twice per day. In low-stakes cases, general and less intense behaviors like compliance and peer interaction (however they are operationally defined) may be most efficiently tracked using a teacher rating form, such as the DBRC. In addition, teachers may be able to monitor frequent behaviors (e.g., a student's call-outs) over a brief, predetermined period of time (e.g., 20 minutes). Direct observation methods also depend on the type of behavior being assessed. For example, infrequent though intense behaviors (e.g., tantrums) may be documented using a behavior log, whereas behaviors that occur more frequently may be recorded by teaching staff or an observer. Table 5.2 provides general guidelines for selecting a monitoring procedure based on the target behavior.

The next section provides a more in-depth review and sample forms for a variety of direct and indirect methods of assessing and monitoring behavior. We begin with direct observation techniques, including event-based and time-based recording techniques, and then follow with indirect methods. As noted previously, forms for all techniques are provided at the end of the chapter.

TABLE 5.2

Selecting and Using an Assessment and Monitoring Technique

Referral Reason	Possible Measurement Technique
Academic concern:	Curriculum-based assessment
	Tests, quizzes, work samples
Behavioral concern:	
Low-stakes behavior	Indirect method (e.g., daily behavior report card)
	Teacher-directed method (e.g., frequency count)
High-stakes behavior	
Specific, high-frequency	Direct observation (independent observer)
	• Time sampling (continuous behaviors)
	• Frequency count (discrete behaviors)
Specific, low-frequency	Behavior log, scatterplot

Direct Observation Techniques

Observed behaviors are considered to be either continuous (having meaningful duration, e.g., being off-task or out of seat) or discrete (having a sudden onset and offset, e.g., calling out, kicking) (Saudargas & Lentz, 1986). Direct observation techniques, then, fall into two categories: *event-based* and *time-based* (Wolery, Bailey, & Sugai, 1988). Discrete behaviors with a clear onset and offset are best recorded with an event-based technique, which records data such as rate or number of times behavior occurs. Examples of event-based techniques include narrative ABC (antecedent-behavior-consequence) records and frequency counts. In contrast, continuous behaviors with meaningful duration are best monitored with a time-based technique such as interval sampling. During interval sampling, data are recorded during specified intervals of time and then summarized as the percentage of intervals during which the behavior occurred.

Event-Based Recording

As noted, event-based techniques are best used when the behavior is discrete, having a relatively clear onset and offset. Generally, these techniques count each occurrence of the behavior. Thus consideration of when the behavior is most likely to occur is important when selecting observation times. The following paragraphs discuss three event-based observation techniques: the narrative ABC record, frequency count, and behavior log and scatterplot procedures.

Narrative ABC record. A narrative record can take many different forms, from a simple global description of an event ("Johnny kicked the teacher during recess") to a narrow and specific description ("During recess today, Johnny kicked the teacher after she told him his turn on the swing was over"). Despite the level of detail in the narrative ABC record, all information presented should be low inference ("Johnny kicked the teacher") rather than high inference ("Johnny got mad at the teacher"). In general, the more complete the description of the behavioral event, the more useful the information is in generating reasons for its occurrence. As its name implies, the Narrative ABC Record (Worksheet 5.1) focuses on information describing the complete behavioral event, beginning with what is occurring in the setting before (antecedents) and after the behavior (consequences) as well as the actual behavior. At the end of the observation, a summary can be developed, listing the frequency of the various behaviors observed, as well as their antecedents and consequences. Although the Narrative ABC Record is easy to complete and provides a great deal of detailed information, it also can be time-consuming, particularly when one attempts to summarize and quantify the information gleaned from multiple observations. For this reason, the ABC format is perhaps most useful to record baseline levels and conditions influencing displayed behavior. Afterward, a more streamlined frequency count procedure might be implemented to monitor and evaluate designed interventions.

Frequency count. A frequency count technique simply entails counting the behavior each time it occurs during the observation period (e.g., counting the number of times Susie disrupts instruction by making an animal noise). An observer may count the identified behavior and record occurrences by using paper and pencil. Alternatives that may be easier to manage include having the classroom teacher or a paraprofessional record behaviors by using a golf-stroke counter or by placing several rubber bands on one wrist and then moving one to the other wrist each time the behavior occurs. Then total number of times, or rate of the occurrence, can be quantitatively summarized (e.g., number of call-outs per 45-minute instructional period) and even easily graphed. Although its simplicity is appealing, this technique also comes at a cost in that the richness of obtained information (setting events, triggers, duration, and intensity of behavior) is limited. Therefore, frequency counts are often used subsequent to other procedures, such as the ABC narrative or scatterplot, or to track moderate- to low-intensity behaviors that occur frequently. Serious behaviors that are less frequent but more intense (e.g., tantrums, fighting) are more adequately documented with the behavior log and scatterplot procedures, next described.

Behavior log and scatterplot. The behavior log and scatterplot procedures are useful when documenting serious behavioral incidents. Using the Behavior Log (Worksheet 5.2), the practitioner collects information about each episode, including the date and time it occurred, the setting and activity, observed triggers, and specific information about the behavior (frequency, duration, and intensity). In addition, the Behavior Scatterplot (Worksheet 5.3) may be used to help determine patterns in the identified behaviors. To complete the form, the practitioner simply draws an X over the space that corresponds to the time and day of each behavioral episode. Afterward, he or she superimposes the student's schedule on the scatterplot to see if any patterns emerge—do certain days, times, activities, settings, or people predict the negative behavior? In addition to establishing baseline levels and monitoring progress toward goals, then, the scatterplot procedure can provide information that is helpful during the problem identification and analysis stages to pinpoint conditions that predict or maintain a given behavior and to inform intervention design by targeting intervention components toward the most prevalent predictors, problematic times and settings, and so on.

Interval Sampling

Interval sampling, a time-based technique, is helpful for tracking continuous behaviors (those without a clear beginning or end), such as pouting, and those that have a meaningful duration, such as being on or off-task or in or out of seat. As its name implies, interval sampling involves breaking an observation period into specified intervals. Behaviors exhibited during each interval are coded, and then a summary of the behaviors across intervals is tallied (percent of intervals in which behavior was observed). Practitioners may use a simple global rating system, such as on-task (+) or off-task (-), or they may use specific codes for multiple behaviors—for example, O: out of seat; L: looking around; and D: disruptive behavior. As already noted, interval sampling works best for observation of behaviors of meaningful duration. However, as the observer becomes more skilled, he or she will also be able to code discrete behaviors (e.g., incidents of paper throwing) observed during each interval. When using interval sampling, the length of the observation period must be predetermined. Usually, observation intervals are 30 seconds or less. In addition, decisions about when to observe and code the behavior will depend on the particular interval sampling technique that has been selected—whole interval, partial interval, or momentary time sampling. Each of these three techniques is discussed further in the following paragraphs.

Whole interval. Whole interval recording involves noting the behavior *only* if it occurs continuously throughout the entire (i.e., whole) interval. For example, in order to mark Cindy's self-verbalization behavior as occurring during a 30-second interval, she must speak during the entire 30 seconds of the interval. Generally, shorter intervals (e.g., 10 seconds) are recommended, given the stringent requirement that the behavior occur through the entire interval. Also, because this technique requires continuous observation, the number of behaviors to observe in a single session must be limited. Perhaps the most significant caution with whole interval recording is that it can *underestimate* the true occurrence of the behavior—again, related to the need for the continuous presence of the behavior in order to record its presence during the interval. Because of this potential for underestimating challenging behavior, whole interval recording may be considered a conservative measurement technique. It has limited use for the purposes of developing implementation plans.

Partial interval. In contrast to whole interval recording, partial interval recording involves marking the behavior as present if it occurs *at any time* during the interval, regardless of how long the behavior continues. For example, if Cindy is out of her seat for 1 second during the 20-second interval, that interval is coded to show that the behavior did occur. Given this requirement, this technique is a better choice than whole interval when the behavior is potentially of low frequency, such as leaving a seat. However, caution is needed with partial interval recording, too: It may *overestimate* the true occurrence of the behavior because it is recorded if it occurs for any portion (even one second) during an interval.

Momentary time sampling. Although similar to both whole and partial interval recording in that behavior is observed during specified intervals, momentary time sampling is different because behavior is coded only at a specified period during the interval, such as at the beginning or end of it. That is, the behavior is coded as occurring (or not) only at the specified interval mark. The main advantage of this procedure is that it is easier to record numerous behaviors simultaneously or to observe more than one student because the time between each momentary interval mark can be allotted to recording the information. This technique is useful when the behavior occurs at a moderate yet steady rate (e.g., vocal tics). Research on the use of momentary time sampling versus whole and partial interval recording has suggested that it may provide a more accurate estimate of true occurrence (Saudargas & Lentz, 1986).

The Interval Sampling Recording Form (Worksheet 5.4), allows for both momentary time sampling to code on-task and off-task behavior and either whole or partial interval recording to code specific behaviors. Directions for the use of each technique are included on the form. Meanwhile, Table 5.3 summarizes observational coding procedures.

Indirect Techniques

As noted earlier, indirect monitoring techniques are more desirable in lower stakes cases and in tracking more general behaviors, like cooperation, participation, and respecting others. Indirect methods are usually less time-consuming and require fewer resources. However, they are also more subjective in nature, less empirically supported, and less accurate.

Self-Report or Ratings by Others

One category of indirect techniques involves ratings by self or others. Generally, a person provides an account of the behavior at a point after it has already occurred (e.g., later in the day or week, over the past month). Techniques include any informal or standardized rating scale, or even questionnaires completed or answered during an interview format. A potential problem with many of the rating scales that are commercially available is inability to use them repeatedly over time due to the length of time needed for their completion and violation of the standardization for administration—in other words, repeating the scale over too brief a period of time. In addition, the global nature of many of these scales may not allow provision of useful information about the specific behavior of concern. In contrast, although informally created scales may address the problem of specificity and frequency of use, the lack of psychometric evidence to support them can be of concern. Despite these cautions, the use of indirect techniques can be beneficial in certain situations.

Daily Behavior Report Card

One indirect monitoring technique that can be used repeatedly is the Daily Behavior Report Card, or DBRC. With the DBRC, one person rates a specified behavior on a daily basis and then shares that information with someone else (Chafouleas, Riley-Tillman, & McDougal, 2002). The DBRC can be individualized to meet the specific needs of a situation, and ratings of specific behaviors can be graphed across time. A Daily Behavior Report Card (Worksheet 5.5) and a form for graphing daily reports over time (Worksheet 5.6) appear at the end of the chapter.

The DBRC is appealing because it is not only useful in monitoring behavior but also can be an important piece of the intervention, particularly if incentives and consequences based on the ratings are added. In addition, a review of the limited literature available on the school-based use of the DBRC suggests that it is feasible, acceptable, and effective in promoting positive behavior and that it increases communication among various concerned parties (e.g., home and school). A form for graphing the daily reports over time is given as Worksheet 5.6.

Nevertheless, an extensive literature base supporting the use of these reports does not yet exist. A further concern with the DBRC is that it is indirect; the rating may not necessarily occur at the time and place of the actual behavior. One way to minimize this problem is to rate the behavior immediately after the observation period. In sum, the DBRC does appear to be a feasible technique for use in the schools, although some caution should be taken in interpreting the information it provides.

Putting It All Together

The selection and use of an appropriate technique for measuring behavior is essential to assess and monitor behavior and to evaluate change. Many considerations are involved in selecting a technique, including determining the type of information needed and weighing the costs and benefits of one technique over another. This chapter has reviewed the reasons for measuring behavior and described several different types of monitoring techniques.

TABLE 5.3

Summary of Observational Coding Procedures

Method	Brief Descriptor	Sample Behavior	Strengths/Weaknesses
EVENT-BASED RECORDING			
Narrative ABC Record	Narrative descriptor of entire behavioral event completed at time of occurrence	Disruptive classroom behavior	*Strengths* Few recording rules Provides detailed information on the conditions influencing behavior Good for problem analysis and for frequently occurring behaviors *Weaknesses* Can be time-consuming Not well-suited for assessing infrequent behaviors or for monitoring over time
Behavior Log	Narrative descriptor of behavioral event completed soon after its occurrence	Physical aggression	*Strengths* Well-suited for documenting and monitoring infrequent but intense behavioral episodes Provides detailed information on the conditions influencing behavior Can be combined with scatterplot technique for problem analysis of behavioral episodes *Weaknesses* Documentation can be time-consuming Not well-suited for assessing frequently occurring behaviors
Behavioral Scatterplot	Technique for analyzing behavior log entries	Physical aggression, tantrums	*Strengths* Provides detailed information on the conditions influencing behavior Good for assessing the influence of variables related to time, day, setting, people, activity, and schedule

TABLE 5.3 (continued)

Method	Brief Descriptor	Sample Behavior	Strengths/Weaknesses
			Weaknesses Assessment can be time-consuming Not designed for monitoring behavior over time
Frequency	Recording that behavior either did or did not occur	Number of verbal disruptions in a 10-minute period	*Strengths* Simple to use Easy to graph
			Weaknesses Provides little information on duration/ intensity of behavior Not suited for continuous or infrequently occurring behaviors
Duration	Recording the length of time the behavior occurs	Length of a temper tantrum	*Strength* Measure of elapsed time
			Weakness Not good for baviors without clear onset/ ending
Latency	Recording the length of time between a signal and the response to the signal	Length of time between request to put books away and books put away	
INTERVAL SAMPLING			
Whole interval	Behavior is recorded if occurring throughout entire interval	Social isolation on the playground	*Strength* Can be used with continuous behaviors
			Weaknesses Can underestimate true occurrence of behavior Not appropriate for infrequent behavior
Partial interval	Behavior is recorded if occurring during any part of the interval	Verbal aggression	*Strength* Good for use with low-frequency yet lengthy behaviors
			Weaknesses Can overestimate true occurrence of behavior

| Momentary time sampling | Coding behavior at specified interval marks | Out of seat, looking out the window | *Strengths* Allows numerous behaviors to be observed simultaneously Provides time to record, easy to conduct peer comparisons |
| | | | *Weaknesses* Could miss infrequently occurring behavior |

It should be noted that many of the direct observation techniques described are appropriate for use in self-monitoring. Self-monitoring of behavior as it occurs is considered a direct technique, and it has been found to be a powerful aid to intervention. However, when students self-monitor, adult supervision is usually required to ensure accurate reporting.

Although this chapter includes only printed forms for the techniques reviewed, it may be worth exploring the growing number of computer-based direct observation programs. Evidence of the quality, usefulness, and acceptability of these programs remains scarce to date, but more information will likely soon be available as new software is developed.

Narrative ABC Record

Student _____   Date/Time _____

Setting _____   Observer _____

Complete a narrative account of the situation, using the boxes below. For each behavior observed, record what happened immediately before (antecedents) and after (consequences) each behavior. Note that sometimes a consequence leads directly to another behavior.

ANTECEDENTS	BEHAVIORS	CONSEQUENCES

From *Functional Behavioral Assessment and Intervention in Schools: A Practitioner's Guide (Grades 1–8)*, by J. L. McDougal, S. M. Chafouleas, and B. Waterman, 2006, Champaign, IL: Research Press (800-519-2707; www.researchpress.com)

Behavior Log

Student _____ Observer _____

Date _____ Time _____ ❑ A.M. ❑ P.M. Setting _____

For each incident, describe the following: what happened, who was involved, what activity was going on, what triggered the incident, and what the outcome was.

1. Description of incident _____

_____

Duration _____ minutes   Intensity ❑ low ❑ medium ❑ high

Was time-out required? ❑ Yes ❑ No   If so, for how long? _____ minutes

Comments _____

_____

2. Description of incident _____

_____

Duration _____ minutes   Intensity ❑ low ❑ medium ❑ high

Was time-out required? ❑ Yes ❑ No   If so, for how long? _____ minutes

Comments _____

_____

3. Description of incident _____

_____

Duration _____ minutes   Intensity ❑ low ❑ medium ❑ high

Was time-out required? ❑ Yes ❑ No   If so, for how long? _____ minutes

Comments _____

_____

4. Description of incident _____

_____

Duration _____ minutes   Intensity ❑ low ❑ medium ❑ high

Was time-out required? ❑ Yes ❑ No   If so, for how long? _____ minutes

Comments _____

_____

From *Functional Behavioral Assessment and Intervention in Schools: A Practitioner's Guide (Grades 1–8)*, by J. L. McDougal, S. M. Chafouleas, and B. Waterman, 2006, Champaign, IL: Research Press (800-519-2707; www.researchpress.com)

Behavioral Scatterplot

Student _____   Dates _____ to _____

Setting _____   Observer _____

Place an X in the space that corresponds to the time and date of each observed behavioral incident. Superimpose the student's daily schedule on the scatterplot and look for clusters of behavioral incidents suggesting meaningful patterns. Attempt to match behaviors to possible influences related to time of day, settings, academic tasks, level of adult supervision, and other instructional or environmental variables.

Dates   _____ _____ _____ _____ _____

	Monday	Tuesday	Wednesday	Thursday	Friday	Comments
8:00 A.M.						
8:15						
8:30						
8:45						
9:00						
9:15						
9:30						
9:45						
10:00						
10:15						
10:30						
10:45						
11:00						
11:15						
11:30						
11:45						
12:00 P.M.						
12:15						
12:30						
12:45						
1:00						
1:15						
1:30						
1:45						
2:00						
2:15						
2:30						
2:45						
3:00						
3:15						
3:30						

From *Functional Behavioral Assessment and Intervention in Schools: A Practitioner's Guide (Grades 1–8)*, by J. L. McDougal, S. M. Chafouleas, and B. Waterman, 2006, Champaign, IL: Research Press (800-519-2707; www.researchpress.com)

WORKSHEET 5.4

Interval Sampling Recording Form

Student _____   Date/Time _____

Teacher _____   Observer _____

Observation Activity _____

White Boxes: Momentary time sampling procedures will be used to code on-task (+) or off-task (-) behavior. Using a stopwatch, observe target student and a same-sex peer and record the observed behavior *at the beginning* of each 20-second interval. (Record target student observation data first.) Compute the percentage of time on task by adding the number of plusses (+) divided by 30 and multiplying by 100 (plusses/30 × 100).

Shaded Boxes: Partial or whole interval recording will be used to code additional specific behaviors of interest. It is recommended that the observer develop a coding system prior to beginning the observation (e.g., noncompliance = C, negative peer interaction = P) and that the number of behaviors (codes) be limited to those of greatest interest. In whole-interval recording, mark the code in the interval if the behavior occurs throughout the entire 20-second interval. In partial-interval recording, enter the code if that behavior occurs *at any point* during the interval. Indicate the behavior codes at the bottom as well as the number of times each behavior occurred for the target and peer.

Interval	1		2		3		4		5		6		7		8	
Target																
Peer																

Interval	9		10		11		12		13		14		15		16	
Target																
Peer																

Interval	17		18		19		20		21		22		23		24	
Target																
Peer																

Interval	25		26		27		28		29		30	
Target												
Peer												

Summary/Codes _____

From *Functional Behavioral Assessment and Intervention in Schools: A Practitioner's Guide (Grades 1–8)*, by J. L. McDougal, S. M. Chafouleas, and B. Waterman, 2006, Champaign, IL: Research Press (800-519-2707; www.researchpress.com)

Daily Behavior Report Card (DBRC)

Student _____ Date _____

Teacher/Rater _____

Compared with other students of the same gender in the classroom, today the student:

1. Completed assigned schoolwork.

1	2	3	4	5
Never	Occasionally	Sometimes	Often	Always

2. Complied with adult requests readily and without argument or complaint.

1	2	3	4	5
Never	Occasionally	Sometimes	Often	Always

3. Interacted appropriately with classmates.

1	2	3	4	5
Never	Occasionally	Sometimes	Often	Always

4. Other behavior: _____

1	2	3	4	5
Never	Occasionally	Sometimes	Often	Always

5. Other behavior: _____

1	2	3	4	5
Never	Occasionally	Sometimes	Often	Always

Rating key: 1 to 2 = poor behavior, 3 = fair behavior, 4 to 5 = good to great behavior

From *Functional Behavioral Assessment and Intervention in Schools: A Practitioner's Guide (Grades 1–8)*, by J. L. McDougal, S. M. Chafouleas, and B. Waterman, 2006, Champaign, IL: Research Press (800-519-2707; www.researchpress.com)

DBRC Graphing Form

Student _____ Dates _____ to _____

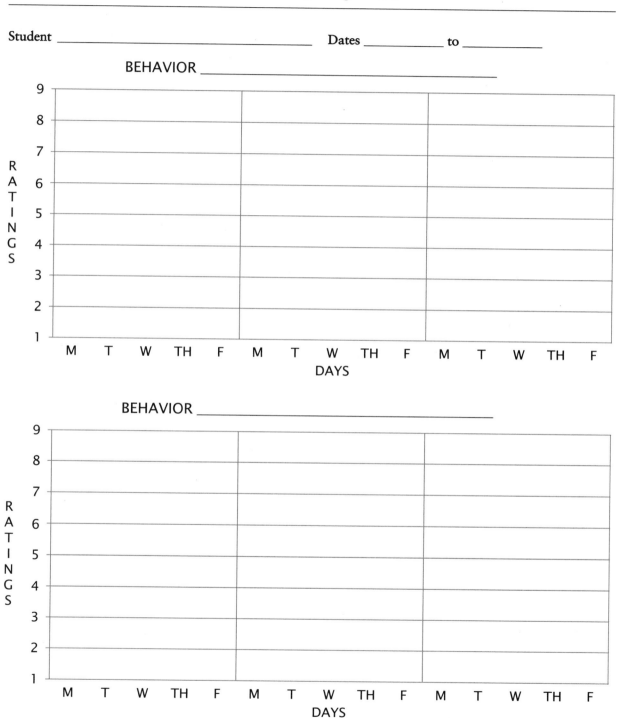

From *Functional Behavioral Assessment and Intervention in Schools: A Practitioner's Guide (Grades 1–8)*, by J. L. McDougal, S. M. Chafouleas, and B. Waterman, 2006, Champaign, IL: Research Press (800-519-2707; www.researchpress.com)

Monitoring Summary Sheet

Student _____   Teacher _____

Target behavior(s) _____

_____

Goal(s) _____

_____

Type of monitoring information collected _____

Preintervention (Baseline) Information

Date/Time	Student Data	Peer Comparison Data

Monitoring Information

Date/Time	Student Data	Peer Comparison Data

Comments _____

_____

From *Functional Behavioral Assessment and Intervention in Schools: A Practitioner's Guide (Grades 1–8)*, by J. L. McDougal, S. M. Chafouleas, and B. Waterman, 2006, Champaign, IL: Research Press (800-519-2707; www.researchpress.com)

Intervention Plan Development and Implementation

Goals for Joey's intervention were to decrease Joey's tantrums to no more than one per week and to increase teacher ratings of compliance to 3 (out of 5) or higher within four weeks. To achieve these goals, multiple components were selected for Joey's intervention plan. The first included antecedent manipulations and preventative strategies, whereby the teacher provided increased cues for task transitions and ignored Joey's quiet noncompliance instead of risking a tantrum by pressing him. Next, a teaching and support strategy was provided, with a fifth-grade peer tutor being assigned to help Joey 30 minutes a day with reading and writing tasks. Consequent strategies included a reinforcement and self-monitoring plan implemented for following teacher directions. After each scheduled interval (eight per day), the teacher would briefly meet with Joey to assess whether he had complied with teacher requests. If Joey and his teacher determined that he had been compliant, Joey earned a positive rating for that period and received teacher praise. At the end of the day, if he earned six out of eight positive ratings (and had no tantrums), he was allowed to go to the cafeteria to have a snack and help the lunch monitors wash tables—a task he enjoyed that also allowed him some positive individual time with adults. Finally, as a home component, the teacher sent home a "good job" note each day to communicate that Joey had met his behavioral goals. The intervention was monitored with a Daily Behavior Report Card (DBRC) for compliance and a teacher log for tantrums. A plan review meeting was scheduled in three weeks' time.

When the assessment piece of the FBA process is complete, the next stage is to move on to designing and implementing an intervention. Each stage completed thus far has implications for intervention design. During the problem identification stage, a target behavior is selected and defined, and a baseline level of functioning is established as a basis for comparison in gauging intervention effectiveness. In the investigation and analysis stage, background information is collected, the conditions that predict the target behavior are identified, skill deficits and communicative intent are assessed, a functional theory is developed, the student's personal strengths and interests are explored, and potential replacement behaviors are identified. To use all this information to guide the creation of an intervention, Mace, Lalli, and Lalli (1991) suggest: "The general strategy [in intervention design] is to alter the environment so as to minimize the reinforcement for aberrant behavior and, whenever possible, provide reinforcement for adaptive responses to compete with maladaptive behavior" (p. 173).

In this chapter, we will cover three basic strategies for altering problem behavior in the school setting: (a) modifying predictive conditions to reduce problem

TABLE 6.1

Stage 3: Intervention Plan Development and Implementation

Stage 1: Problem Identification

Stage 2: Problem Investigation and Analysis

Stage 3: Intervention Plan Development and Implementation

- Link assessment to intervention.
- Select an intervention technique.
- Develop the behavior intervention plan and begin implementation.

Stage 4: Intervention Plan Evaluation

behavior and support replacement behaviors, (b) teaching skills the student does not possess or supporting the student in performing positive behaviors at a higher rate, and (c) altering the consequences so that desired replacement behaviors become more functional than the problem behaviors. Each of these strategies should be discussed in depth as an intervention plan is developed and implemented. Table 6.1 outlines the tasks to accomplish during this stage.

Link Assessment to Intervention

Our discussion of linking assessment information to intervention design is based on a competing behaviors pathway model (see Gresham, Watson, & Skinner, 2001; O'Neill et al., 1997). We believe this model helps organize FBA assessment information in a way that informs intervention design. A key concept underlying this model is that problem behaviors successfully "compete" with more desirable behaviors because they are easier to exhibit (more efficient) and reliably result in the desired (maintaining) consequence. Therefore, interventions should be designed to (a) change predictive conditions (i.e., antecedent and setting variables) to decrease the likelihood of problematic behavior; (b) teach prosocial replacement behaviors and address skill deficits (through direct instruction, modeling, practice opportunities, and feedback); and (c) alter consequent events so that replacement behaviors are functionally reinforced and problem behaviors become irrelevant (are no longer needed), inefficient (take too much effort), and ineffective (no longer result in the maintaining consequence).

As Figure 6.1 shows, the competing pathways model has three parts: the predictive conditions that are believed to influence the problem behavior, the behaviors of interest, and the consequences that maintain the behaviors. Once these pieces are diagrammed, it is possible to generate suggestions for interventions that target one or more of these areas. The predictive conditions piece of the intervention gener-

FIGURE 6.1

Linking Assessment to Intervention through the Competing Pathways Model

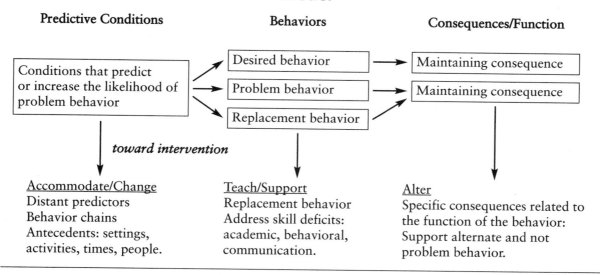

ally focuses on accommodations or manipulations of identified antecedents, whereas ideas for addressing selected behaviors emphasize teach-and-support strategies. Finally, consequent strategies are developed to alter the behavioral outcome so that the reinforcement of problem behavior is diminished and alternative replacement behavior becomes more functional.

Figure 6.2 illustrates the step-by-step process for completing the Assessment-to-Intervention Worksheet. The top half of the diagram is completed based on assessment information taken from the completed Functional Behavioral Assessment Worksheet. A blank version of this worksheet appears in Appendix A.

In Step 1, the problem or target behavior is listed in the *behaviors* section. Under *consequences/function*, the consequences that seem to motivate or maintain the student's behavior (e.g., being sent to the office) are noted, along with the hypothesized function (e.g., escaping an unpleasant task). For each problem behavior, a replacement behavior (a more positive behavior that serves a similar function) and a desired behavior are identified. The desired behavior is included to illustrate that the maintaining consequence is different from that supporting the problem (and replacement) behaviors.

Step 2 requires documenting the previously identified conditions that predict the occurrence of the problem behavior. In the *predictive conditions* section, the information previously gathered on distant predictors, precursor behaviors and behavior chains; general antecedents; and problematic settings and activities is listed. This information will provide important preventative considerations for intervention

FIGURE 6.2

Assessment-to-Intervention Worksheet

Student _____ Grade _____ Date _____

ASSESSMENT INFORMATION

Predictive Conditions	Behaviors	Consequences/Function
Distant:	Desired:	
Precursor behaviors:		
Step 2 List predictive conditions	Problem:	
	Replacement:	**Step 1** Diagram behaviors
Antecedents:		

→   →   →

INTERVENTION COMPONENTS

Prevention	Teaching/Support	Alter Consequences
Distant:	Address skill deficits:	New consequences for problem behaviors:
Step 3 Prevent/accommodate predictive conditions	**Step 4** Address skill deficits/teach and support replacement behaviors	**Step 5** Alter consequences: Support replacement behavior, make problem behavior inefficient and ineffective
Precursor behaviors:	Teach replacement behaviors:	
Antecedents:		Reinforcement and monitoring ideas to promote replacement behaviors:

design. Once this assessment portion of the diagram is completed, it is time to move on to the bottom half of the diagram, which requires the brainstorming of potential intervention components.

Step 3 involves creating a *prevention* plan by developing strategies, accommodations, and alterations to the environment to diminish the influence of the identified predictive conditions. Ideas for addressing each of the predictors—distant, precursor behaviors, and antecedents—are included here.

Step 4, *teaching and support,* involves making a plan to address any skill deficits identified in the assessment stage and to teach and support replacement behaviors.

Last, Step 5 involves developing some ideas to *alter consequences* to support replacement behaviors and ensure that problem behaviors no longer effectively or efficiently maintain consequences.

Figure 6.3 illustrates how these steps are applied. The example shown is for Donna, a fifth-grade student referred for intervention services for refusing to do classwork and for incidents of yelling and swearing when pressed to comply. During the assessment stage, the FBA worksheet was completed to document baseline levels of these behaviors in addition to important information about antecedents and consequences. The functional theory developed for Donna states that "When independent seatwork demands occur in the context of afternoon math class, Donna displays refusal and/or yelling/swearing behavior in order to escape the task, and these target behaviors may be related to poor math skills." In addition, these episodes were believed to be more likely when Donna was tired or moody. Because avoiding personally difficult independent work in math appeared to be the maintaining consequence, replacement behaviors identified included requesting two-minute breaks, providing a peer learning partner, and focusing on completing modified assignments. Teaching and support ideas were developed to provide academic support in math and to instruct and promote the alternative behaviors. Further, prevention planning focused on altering Donna's schedule and changing educators' responses to Donna when she was tired and moody. Last, ideas for altering the consequences of Donna's behavior included not sending her to the office for task refusal, allowing her two-minute breaks, and reinforcing and monitoring her completion of modified tasks with a peer.

Select Intervention Components

As already noted, there are three targets for change in a problem-behavior intervention: (a) modifying the conditions that predict the behavior; (b) directly teaching or supporting the skills the student does not possess or does not often perform; and (c) altering the consequences so that replacement behaviors become more functional than problem behaviors. The following discussion expands on these components.

FIGURE 6.3

Sample Assessment-to-Intervention Worksheet

Student ___Donna___   Grade ___8___   Date ___2/7/06___

ASSESSMENT INFORMATION

Predictive Conditions	Behaviors	Consequences/Function
Distant: *Unknown*	**Desired:** *On-task, complete independent seatwork*	*Academic success, positive attention*
Precursor behaviors: *Tired looking, moody*	**Problem:** *Task refusal, swears and yells when pressed*	*Redirected, sent to office, avoids independent math tasks*
Antecedents: *Difficult task, independent seatwork, math, afternoon time*	**Replacement:** *Complete modified tasks, request breaks, use peer support*	*Avoids independent math tasks*

INTERVENTION COMPONENTS

Prevention	Teaching/Support	Alter Consequences
Distant: *None*	**Address skill deficits:** *Instruct in the use of monitoring and reinforcement plan*	New consequences for problem behaviors: *Task refusal does not result in office referral; two-minute break requests honored*
Precursor behaviors: *Acknowledge tiredness and give extra space, response time, and choice of tasks*	**Teach replacement behaviors:**	*Reinforcement and monitoring ideas to promote replacement behaviors:*
Antecedents: *Alter schedule (math in the morning), modify tasks (intersperse easy and hard items), increase academic support (learning partner)*	• *To request two-minute breaks* • *To focus on modified tasks* • *To make use of peer learning partner*	*Correct use of peer and completion of modified tasks to be monitored and reinforced with preferred privilege during task time*

Modify Predictors

In moving from assessment to intervention, we first consider preventative strategies to alter those conditions known to predict or influence problem behavior. This is an important part of being *proactive* rather than *reactive*. This section provides a brief review of some accommodations for distant and more immediate predictors of problem behavior. These are relevant for use in the prevention section of the Assessment-to-Intervention Worksheet shown in Figures 6.2 and 6.3.

Distant Predictors

Information from a variety of sources (parents, teachers, bus driver, administrators, and so forth) is used at this point to address influences on negative behavior that do not occur in direct proximity to the behavior. For example, a student who is harassed on the school bus or in the hallway may have behavior problems later in the classroom. Such previously identified distant predictors will be addressed or modified in the intervention plan—for the harassed student, this might mean a change of seat on the bus or increased supervision in the hallway. Interventions to address other distant predictors might include providing a midmorning snack to address a student's hunger, building a rest period into the student's schedule, monitoring or reviewing medication, or providing a supportive therapeutic intervention to address past trauma. In addition, referral for specialized evaluation may be warranted (e.g., neurological, medical). Although some medical, physiological, and social factors may not reasonably be remediated by the schools directly, many of the problems associated with these factors—hunger or the need to talk to a caring adult, for example—are feasible accommodations to be made in school. In addition, having some background information may help evaluators compile a list of home and community supports available to the student and family to promote a more accommodating environment outside of school.

Precursor Behaviors

Recall the earlier discussion on behavior chains: smaller behaviors that tend to occur prior to more intense episodes. Modifying our response to the first identifiable precursor behavior in these chains may be an important preventative component of an individual intervention. For example, a first-grade boy was noted to become flushed in the face and slouch down in his chair prior to tantrum episodes. Using these precursor signs, school staff developed proactive measures, including visiting with a preferred adult or a brief walk in the hall, to be implemented when these behavioral signs appeared, prior to a full-blown tantrum. In this case, attending to and intervening with lower level behaviors avoided more intense behavioral episodes. Therefore, when precursor behaviors are identified in the FBA they are included on the Assessment-to-Intervention Worksheet, and a prevention or accommodation strategy is developed.

Immediate Predictors

During the assessment stage of the FBA process, the more immediate environmental conditions and behaviors that appear to predict each target behavior are identified. These include general antecedents and problematic settings, activities, and people that seem to be related to the target behavior. Moving from assessment to intervention requires that these related variables be modified in order to reduce the likelihood of problematic behavior.

General antecedents. After consideration of any behavior chains, the intervention process proceeds to modifying antecedents in proximity to the behavior. General antecedents, or triggers, to negative behavior in school may include a lack of teacher attention, the presence of certain people (staff or students), a difficult task, and an interruption in routine or abrupt transitions from one task to another. Appropriate responses to these triggers might be to increase praise statements, reduce exposure to certain staff members, modify the length or duration of academic tasks, structure transitions, or avoid interruptions in routine or cue students prior to interruptions when possible. General ideas for antecedent manipulation include changing the student's schedule, altering the size and composition of groups, shortening tasks, mixing easy and difficult tasks, offering reminders for expected behaviors, modifying the curriculum, and providing breaks to the student (see Gresham, Watson, & Skinner, 2001; Sprague, Sugai, & Walker, 1998). Table 6.2 offers specific ideas for addressing identified antecedents.

Settings and activities. Although they are technically also antecedents to problematic behavior, the settings and activities in which behaviors occur are listed separately on the worksheet shown in Figures 6.2 and 6.3. When behavioral assessment highlights specific settings or activities that reliably predict problem behavior, the intervention design process becomes more focused. Along with direct observation and interview information, the scatterplot technique (described in chapter 5) has been a particularly useful tool for identifying settings, times, and activities in which target behaviors, especially high-intensity/low-frequency behaviors, are likely to occur. For example, problematic settings may include the cafeteria, hallway, special classes, and classes with specific instructors. Predictive activities in those settings might include independent seatwork, group instruction, specific academic subjects, class lectures, and unstructured academic downtime. When these settings, times, and activities are identified, modification of those variables can occur. The goal is to structure the child's environment to reduce the incidents of problem behavior. Based on assessment results, for example, access to a loud and crowded cafeteria might be reduced, unstructured time could be transformed to independent reading time, and class lectures might be reduced by implementing cooperative learning assignments.

Address Skill Deficits and Communicative Intent

The point of teaching and support strategies is to develop skills that are not currently in the student's repertoire or to promote skills that the student possesses but does not reliably perform. These strategies first focus on instructional practices to address identified skill deficits in the areas of academics, behavior, and communication. The goal is to find specific replacement behaviors while teaching the required skills and providing modeling and support for the student to exhibit the skills in the desired context. Once

<u>**TABLE 6.2**</u>

Manipulating Antecedents

Identified Antecedent	Modification
Lack of adult attention	Use praise systematically.
Teacher demand or request	Allow student choice; provide wait time; practice planned ignoring.
Specific academic task	Modify assignment; use a learning buddy.
Transitions (task or setting)	Structure and practice transitions; cue students prior to transitions; review schedule throughout the day.

the student exhibits the skills, they may be supported and promoted by making environmental and curricular modifications, as well as by altering the consequences for these behaviors. We offer general ideas for addressing deficits in academic skills, behavioral skills, and communication in the following paragraphs.

Behavioral Skill Deficits

Behavioral skill deficits are usually addressed through some type of skills training that, in addition to instruction, involves opportunities for modeling, practicing, and reinforcing the learned skills. Such strategies are common in many social skills and anger management training programs. For example, one anger management exercise requires students to identify the factors (triggers) that make them angry, the physiological cues indicating they are becoming angry, and the activities they can engage in to calm down (anger reducers). The teacher can then model the use of these skills during frustrating times. When subsequent student conflict arises in the classroom, the students involved can be prompted to identify their anger and to employ a prespecified anger reducer. Praise, positive social attention, and individually preferred reinforcers may be used to develop the appropriate use of the skill and to promote future use. Chapter 8 provides a number of general intervention strategies to promote positive behavioral skills, including the Survivor Skills and Targeted Skills intervention formats.

Academic Skill Deficits

Academic skill deficits commonly co-occur with problematic behavior, and such deficits may need to be identified and remediated as well. As discussed in chapter 2, the instructional hierarchy has been proposed as one useful model for the development of instructional interventions (Daly, Witt, Martens, & Dool, 1997; Haring, Lovitt, Eaton, & Hansen, 1978; Witt, Daly, & Noell, 2000). The instructional hierarchy illustrates how assessment of the student's stage in the learning process may be directly linked to the type of academic intervention prescribed. For example, a first-grade student noted to be a slow yet accurate reader would probably need a fluency-building intervention. Therefore, the teacher might be asked to pair the student with a slightly better reader to engage each day in a choral reading exercise (when students read in unison), a technique that has been shown to build reading fluency. Chapter 8 outlines a variety of interventions designed to promote academic skill acquisition through the accuracy, fluency, and generalization stages. These strategies are useful in remediating basic skill deficits. However, skill remediation may be secondary; the student may first need curricular modification and peer or teacher support to tackle difficult material.

Communicative Intent

Communicative intent may be involved when the problem behavior appears to be an efficient or reliable means for the child to express a need or desire. Behaviors related to communication are more prevalent in young children and in those with communicative delays. In our experience, preschool and primary-grade students and students with expressive language or cognitive delays are most likely to require communicative interventions. Linking the identified communication difficulty to an intervention involves anticipating the need the child is communicating through the aberrant behavior, creating an environment conducive to communication, and developing a formal functional communication training component for the individual's plan.

For example, a five-year-old girl was referred for tantrum behaviors: crying, yelling, dropping to the floor, and flailing her hands and feet. These tantrums typically occurred within one hour of morning arrival at school. The precursor behaviors noted were facial tension/grimacing, social withdrawal, refusing to work, and hiding her head in her coat; these behaviors were followed by tantrums. The teacher noted that the child would not speak prior to these tantrums and that she had a difficult time expressing her feelings. Based on a significant social history and the fact that the tantrums occurred soon after the child arrived at school, the school psychologist hypothesized that distant predictors included stressors the student was encountering outside of the school environment. The withdrawal and tantrum behaviors might be serving to communicate emotional upset and lack of readiness to engage in the academic schedule. In addition to an instructional and incentive-based plan focusing on behavioral control, the school psychologist added a morning check-in procedure. This procedure involved having the student visit the social worker each morning prior to entering the classroom. If the student appeared calm and could verbalize her thoughts and feelings, she was quickly greeted and sent to class. But if she appeared upset and withdrawn, the social worker provided her with a quiet area to verbalize her feelings and gain the necessary composure to enter the classroom successfully.

Most commonly, communication issues are addressed through functional communication training. This training usually involves teaching the student verbal or nonverbal responses to meet specific assessed needs (e.g., to request a break or communicate hunger). In addition to being taught, the identified phrases or cues are then modeled, prompted, and differentially reinforced to encourage the student to use them. Chapter 8 describes functional communication training procedures as well as other intervention ideas to address communicative needs.

Modify Maintaining Consequences

The identified consequences—not necessarily punitive measures but conditions or responses occurring subsequent to target behaviors—are next considered. At times, it may be possible to transform the consequences into incentives to promote adaptive behavior. For example, a student frequently sent to the office for disruptive classroom behavior might instead be allowed to earn time in the office with an administrator for positive on-task behavior in the classroom.

A key concept involved in linking assessment information to intervention is that of *functional relevance*. After identification of the consequences maintaining a target behavior, the goal is to identify an alternative or competing, and more socially appropriate, behavior that can serve the same function (and thereby is functionally relevant). For example, an intervention for a student believed to be disrupting class in order to gain teacher and peer attention might be self-monitoring. Functional relevance might involve promoting a more appropriate replacement behavior, such as hand raising and staying on task, with "attention-rich" reinforcement opportunities (e.g., assigning a peer tutor or class helper for younger students, allowing the child to become an assistant in the school office). Table 6.3 provides a summary of some intervention techniques, incentives, and consequences based on the hypothesized function of a student's behavior.

Three steps are involved in addressing the suspected function of a problem behavior. First, the teacher is careful not to allow the negative behavior to continue to serve the same function for the student; in other words, the teacher no longer reinforces the target behavior. For example, attention-seeking call-outs may be ignored, or disruptive behavior designed to get the student sent to the office might instead result in the child's completing an independent task in another teacher's room. Second, the identified replacement behavior is clearly explained or taught to the student. This is the positive, more socially appropriate behavior that replaces the negative behavior but serves the same function for the student. Third, this replacement behavior is promoted with a functionally relevant and individually preferred reinforcer (differential reinforcement of the replacement behavior).

The case of Jason, a third grader we met in chapter 4, shows the development of a functionally relevant replacement behavior and reinforcer. As you may recall, Jason played the part of class clown by exhibiting calling-out behavior that was supported by peer and teacher attention. Jason liked to read and was quite social. The intervention for Jason involved a self-monitoring procedure that required him to monitor his call-outs each academic period of the day. If he raised his hand in class and reduced call-outs to no more than three per period, he was allowed to read books to a kindergarten class during the 20 minutes before dismissal. This intervention tapped his strength in reading, reinforced hand-raising and self-monitoring of call-outs with an attention-rich (and functionally relevant) motivator, and provided him with a role

TABLE 6.3

Intervention Ideas by Behavioral Function

Function	Intervention Technique	Incentive Ideas	Consequence Ideas
To get something:			

Attention	Self-monitoring
	Behavior contract
	School-home notes
	Public posting
		Peer tutoring
		Peer mentor
		Office assistant
		Praise
			Planned ignoring
			Brief time-out in
			  another room
			Loss of incentive
			Loss of social time
			  (e.g., recess)

Item, activity, area	Self-monitoring
	Behavior contract
	Response cost
		Access to desired item
		Access to desired area
		Access to desired
		  activity
			Remove access to
			  desired item
			Remove access to
			  desired area
			Remove access to
			  desired activity

Sensory stimulation	Student choice
	Behavior modification
	  plan
	Short on-task intervals
		Koosh ball
		Walkman/preferred
		  music
		Interval of physical
		  activity
			Interrupt automatic
			  reinforcement
			Redirect student to task
			Loss of incentive

To escape something:	Shorten activity/
	  assignment
	Behavior contract
	School-home notes
	Response cost
		Homework pass
		Choice time
		Home-based incentive
		Free-time minutes
			Detention
			Withhold free time until
			  work is complete
			Loss of incentive
			Loss of free-time minutes

in which he could receive positive social attention for responsibility rather than negative attention for irresponsibility.

Develop and Implement the Behavior Intervention Plan

The ultimate goal of the FBA process is to create an individualized student behavior intervention plan (BIP). Upah and Tilly (2002) suggest that relevant intervention components at this stage of the process include goal setting, a clear description of intervention procedures, a measurement/monitoring strategy, and a plan for decision making (including how long the intervention will be implemented and how much data will be collected). Figure 6.4 (on pp. 83–85) shows a sample Behavior Intervention Plan Worksheet. A blank copy of this worksheet is given in Appendix A.

The first section of this worksheet relates to goal setting. As discussed in chapter 5, goals should be observable, measurable, and consistent with the baseline measure and monitoring technique chosen to evaluate student progress. The goals developed should be ambitious yet reasonable in amount of progress expected. A rule of thumb is to expect an effective intervention to decrease a target behavior by roughly half the baseline level within two to four weeks. Here are some examples of effective goal statements:

> Jason will decrease call-outs to three or fewer per academic period within two weeks.

> Lakeshia will reduce tantrums in the classroom to no more than two per week by October 25.

> Stevie will consistently earn daily behavior report card ratings of at least 4 out of 5 (for positive peer interactions) within two weeks.

> Gerry will consistently and accurately rate his class participation and respectful behavior toward others as "great" in four out of six periods per day by the end of the month.

After goals have been set, the next two items on the worksheet require (a) a summary of antecedent and setting manipulations and (b) a description of plans to support identified skill deficits (if applicable). More detailed information may be attached and simply referred to in these sections if necessary. For instance, a protocol for structuring transitions may be attached and referenced in the antecedent/settings section, whereas a specific social skills program might be selected for inclusion in the replacement behaviors and skill deficit section.

Next each step or component of the intervention is described, and additional documentation is attached as necessary. For instance, contingency contracts, self-monitoring forms, and crisis plans could be referred to in this section and then attached. The goal here is to provide a concrete summary of each step or component of the procedural plan. This description should be detailed enough so that a substitute teacher entering the class for the first time could read and implement the procedure.

After the description of the intervention, the next section requires that an intervention monitoring plan be described. First, the plans for monitoring student progress and plan integrity are identified; sample monitoring forms may be attached. The monitoring section should include a statement identifying the frequency with which the monitoring will occur (number of times per hour, day, or week), when the monitoring will occur (e.g., after each scheduled activity, at the end of the day), and the person or persons responsible for monitoring. Again, in order to assist with the decision-making process, the monitoring technique should be consistent with the goal statement and the baseline measure.

Next the worksheet prompts consideration of intervention integrity, or the extent to which the intervention is implemented as planned. Keeping hard copies of self-monitoring or DBRC forms is one feasible technique for checking integrity. The last piece of required information in this section is the number of weeks the plan is to be implemented prior to review and evaluation; two to six weeks are typical.

The sample worksheet is complete: Plan evaluation and the revision of interventions based on monitoring data will be discussed in chapter 7.

Putting It All Together

The main goal of the FBA process is to identify changeable variables that may be used to design effective interventions. This chapter has examined the use of assessment information to guide intervention design. Linking assessment to intervention involves using background information, modifying the conditions that predict target behavior, addressing identified skill deficits and communicative intent, and creating functionally relevant interventions based on the consequences supporting negative behavior and the personal strengths and preferences of the individual. The sample cases presented in Appendix C illustrate one way to carry out the assessment-to-intervention process. Chapter 7 addresses the plan evaluation stage of the behavior intervention process. Here a process will be explained for using the collected monitoring information to inform intervention revision and, ultimately, to assess intervention effectiveness. Chapters 8 through 10 explore general intervention ideas to assist in classroom management as well as individual interventions to address specific functions of behavior commonly seen in school settings.

FIGURE 6.4

Sample Behavior Intervention Plan Worksheet

Student _Joey_ _____ Grade _1_ _____ Date _1/17/06_ _____

Behavioral Goals

State in observable, measurable terms, related to target behaviors.

1. *Reduce tantrums (dropping to the floor, yelling, hitting, etc.) to 1 or less per week within 4 weeks*

2. *Increase teacher ratings of compliance to 3 or more within 4 weeks*

Detail changes made to prevent the problem (antecedent and setting manipulations):
The teacher will:

Provide cues for task transitions (5 minutes, 1 minute).

Ignore quiet or passive noncompliance, although may cue Joey periodically to participate in the lesson.

Indicate teaching and support plan to teach replacement behaviors and address identified skill deficits:

A fifth-grade peer tutor will be assigned to Joey for 30 minutes per day to help him complete assignments.

Joey will be taught how to use the peer tutor and be trained in the self-monitoring, incentive, and home components of this plan.

FIGURE 6.4 (continued)

Intervention Steps/Components

Include each step of the intervention, persons responsible, and where and when it will occur. Attach specific intervention forms as applicable. For each intervention:

- Indicate replacement behaviors/roles and how they will be reinforced.
- Identify new consequences imposed for each negative behavior.
- Include a crisis plan for unsafe behavior (if applicable).

Joey will be assigned a peer tutor and have 30 minutes of access to peer tutoring per day.

The teacher will:

> *Provide cues prior to each task transition and ignore noncompliance.*

> *"Preset" him prior to each self-monitoring interval and review/rate his*
> *behavior after the interval (complete the self-monitoring form).*

> *Give praise for each positive rating.*

> *Allow Joey to go to the cafeteria to get a snack and serve as an assistant*
> *when he gets at least 6 of 8 positive ratings.*

> *Complete the DBRC and behavior log for monitoring.*

> *Send home a "good note" each day Joey earns the incentive.*

Monitoring Student Progress

How will progress be monitored, how often, and by whom?

The teacher will:

> *Complete the DBRC each day to monitor Joey's compliance.*

> *Complete a behavior log to document each tantrum.*

Monitoring Plan Integrity

How will plan implementation be monitored, how often, and by whom?

The teacher will complete a daily integrity checklist to rate how well she provides cues for task
transitions and ignores Joey's quiet or passive noncompliance, and cues him to participate.

Number of instructional weeks before plan will be evaluated ___4___

Plan Evaluation

Indicate student progress toward identified goals.

Joey has successfully reduced tantrums to one or less incidents per week.

He has successfully earned DBRC compliance ratings of 3 or higher over the

last week.

Indicate the extent to which the intervention was implemented as designed.

The daily integrity checklist completed by the teacher indicates that each

component of the plan was implemented 90 percent of the time.

How many instructional weeks was the intervention applied?   *4*

Plan Revisions

Indicate any revisions made to the plan.

The plan will continue as designed until the next 4-week follow-up meeting. At that point, we will

consider reducing the number of self-monitoring intervals per day to make the intervention

easier to implement.

Next review date   *3/17/06*

CHAPTER 7

Intervention Plan Evaluation

As described in previous chapters, goals for Joey's intervention were to decrease his tantrums to no more than one per week and to increase teacher ratings of compliance to 3 (out of 5) or higher within four weeks. To assess Joey's progress, his DBRC ratings were collected daily and graphed each week. Study of this graph indicated that Joey's behavior varied initially, but, over the last week of the intervention, Joey consistently earned DBRC ratings of 3s and 4s. In addition, Joey had fewer than one tantrum per week, as recorded on a teacher-monitored behavior log. The peer tutoring was going well, and Joey used that time to get assistance in completing his assignments. A daily integrity checklist completed by the teacher suggested that she was able to implement each component of the designed plan at least 90 percent of the time. Feedback from Joey's aunt suggested that he was proud of the "good job" notes he received. When he brought them home, she displayed them on the refrigerator and gave Joey a small privilege (extra TV or computer time). A follow-up meeting with his teacher suggested that the plan had effectively allowed Joey to improve his behavior in the classroom. At the meeting, it was decided to continue the plan as designed and, at the next follow-up meeting, to consider decreasing the number of monitoring intervals to increase the feasibility of the plan for longer term classroom use.

At this point, the problem identification and investigation stages are complete, and the intervention plan has been designed and implemented. The final stage in the FBA process is the plan evaluation stage. At this stage, progress monitoring results are compared with baseline measures and identified goals to assess the effectiveness of the intervention plan. Plan evaluation addresses whether the intervention is working, whether it is being implemented as designed, and, ultimately, whether it is effective. In this chapter, we will cover requirements for evaluating the effectiveness of the intervention plan. The steps in this process are highlighted in Table 7.1. The following discussion describes each step in the plan evaluation stage; a case example illustrating the entire plan evaluation process in action completes the chapter. A form indicating decision points at each step and guiding this phase of the FBA process is included as Worksheet 7.1, at the end of this chapter.

Assess Intervention Integrity

Because poorly implemented interventions are unlikely to be effective, the first step in the plan evaluation process is to assess the extent to which the intervention is being implemented as designed. There are several practical methods for assessing intervention integrity. The first is to use a daily integrity checklist like the example shown in Figure 7.1. The teacher completes the checklist, rating whether or not he or she applied

TABLE 7.1

Stage 4: Intervention Plan Evaluation

Stage 1: Problem Identification

Stage 2: Problem Investigation

Stage 3: Intervention Plan Development and Implementation

Stage 4: Intervention Plan Evaluation

- Assess intervention integrity.
- Collect and graph progress monitoring results.
- Conduct formative assessment.
- Conduct summative assessment.

each component of the intervention on a given day. In addition, the integrity checklist may serve as a useful guide to train others to implement the intervention. (A blank version of this checklist appears as Worksheet 7.2, at the end of the chapter.)

A second approach to integrity monitoring is to observe the implementation of a designed intervention periodically. The integrity checklist would also be useful for recording the results of observations. In fact, teacher ratings and objective observations can be used to assess the consistency of perceptions regarding intervention implementation and to provide feedback to those implementing it. Perhaps the most efficient, although least accurate, approach to integrity monitoring is to interview the teacher periodically throughout the implementation stage to ascertain whether he or she feels that the intervention is being implemented as designed and continues to be feasible for use in the classroom. This approach should be supplemented with specific ratings and observations when the case is "high stakes" or when concerns are being expressed about the intervention or the student's progress. In some cases, a psychological evaluation (for a potential change of placement) might be conducted, given that the student's behavior significantly interferes with classroom functioning and persists in spite of several appropriately designed interventions implemented over time.

Collect and Graph Progress Monitoring Results

The plan evaluation stage requires that student monitoring results be collected on a frequent basis and graphed periodically for use in the formative assessment process (usually conducted during follow-up meetings). Using graphs to display the data allows the school professional to better present findings to others in a way that encourages and enhances problem-solving models. Graphs are excellent tools for communicating intervention results with teachers, parents, multidisciplinary teams, and other relevant stakeholders. Figure 7.2 is a graph of the results of the intervention plan for Joey.

FIGURE 7.1

Sample Daily Behavior Intervention Checklist

Student ___Joey___ Date___3/16/06___

Teacher/Observer ___Mrs. Robinson___

Intervention(s) ___Prevention, tutoring, self-monitoring, incentive plan___

List each step of the intervention(s). If necessary, add extra spaces. Circle the rating for each step.

1 = I completed this step today.

2 = I partially completed this step today.

3 = I did not complete this step today.

Intervention steps	*Rating scale*
1. *Provided cues for task transitions.*	1 ② 3
2. *Ignored Joey's quiet noncompliance.*	① 2 3
3. *Provided access to 30 minutes of peer tutoring.*	① 2 3
4. *Preset Joey before each monitoring interval and reviewed/rated behavior after.*	① 2 3
5. *Gave incentive when earned.*	① 2 3
6. *Completed DBRC and behavior log for monitoring.*	① 2 3
7. *Sent home "Good Job Note" when earned.*	① 2 3

Comments:

Joey did well today, although I forgot to cue him for transitions a couple of times.

FIGURE 7.2

Results for Joey's Intervention

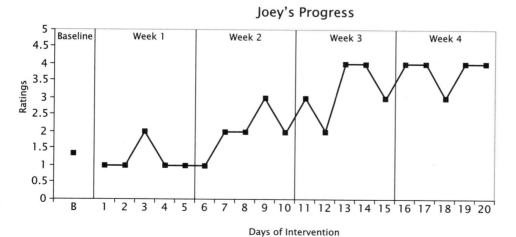

Joey's Progress

Upah and Tilly (2002) highlight three main purposes for which graphs are useful. First, graphs provide a means of visually summarizing information about student performance, projected performance, and actual performance as it changes over the course of an intervention. Graphs provide a visual representation of progress attained, versus that which is projected, and are clear, concise methods for displaying response to intervention. Second, sharing graphed results during the intervention phase may help to shape positive perceptions of intervention effectiveness and student progress. When members of an intervention team are offered visual corroboration that an intervention is producing results, they are more likely to support the intervention and the process. "Such reinforcement helps to maintain the participation of those people in the treatment program, which is critical if objectives are to be achieved" (Sulzer-Azaroff & Mayer, 1991, p. 128). Third, graphing provides a "measure of professional accountability demonstrating how behavior change is functionally related to the intervention being implemented" (Upah & Tilly, 2002, p. 491). Graphs allow teachers and school psychologists to determine when modification of an intervention is necessary or when a new intervention design is most appropriate. Although graphs are only as accurate as the information used to construct them, they are excellent for illustrating student progress and intervention effects.

Typically, graphs include an illustration of the student's baseline performance and progress over the course of the intervention. Several of the techniques for monitoring behavioral performance reviewed in chapter 5 would be appropriate for graphing.

A resource for creating graphs can be found at http://www.oswego.edu/~mcdougal/. On this site is a tool to help school-based professionals graph student monitoring results. The resource, called "Graphing Made Easy," provides visitors with free downloadable graphing templates for the most popular measures of academic and behavioral performance. The templates allow users to select a monitoring technique, fill in student data, and hit a button to create the graph.

Conduct Formative Assessment

Once student monitoring data are collected and graphed, they can be used in the formative assessment process. In this process, the student's progress is compared with baseline levels and predetermined goals to illustrate the extent to which the intervention is having the desired effect and to help guide revision of the intervention, if appropriate. After evaluators ensure that the intervention continues to be feasible for implementation in the classroom, they review the student progress graph in the context of baseline levels and predetermined goals. Based on the amount of progress noted, Worksheet 7.1 directs the practitioner to appropriate plan revision activities. These would range from fading or streamlining intervention components for effective plans to significant revision and a revisiting of assessment information for plans demonstrating limited effect.

One practical approach to decision making at the formative assessment stage is called the *four-point rule* (see Upah & Tilly, 2002). If, on the student progress graph, four consecutive points are at or above the goal line, then the intervention would seem to be working. At this point the intervention planners may consider raising the goal or streamlining or fading the plan for longer term implementation. If four consecutive points fall below the line, the plan may need to be revised by increasing the opportunities to respond or the reinforcement available to support the development of positive behavior. Highly variable data points suggest a need to further motivate the student to consistently meet expectations and/or conduct an intervention integrity check.

The formative assessment process is generally undertaken at predetermined points in time, usually at follow-up meetings that occur every week or two. Prior to the formative assessment process, integrity information has been reviewed to ensure that the intervention is being implemented as designed. In addition, the student progress data have been collected and graphed to inform formative decisions. At this point, the intervention is revised based on student progress information compared to baseline levels and predetermined goals.

Conduct Summative Assessment

Whereas the purpose of the formative assessment process is to revise the intervention plan based on student performance, the purpose of the summative evaluation is to answer the question "Did the intervention work?" After several cycles of formative revision, the intervention planners will need to use the graphic displays of student progress to determine whether or not the student has adequately progressed in the designed intervention.

Summative assessment involves the use of progress-monitoring information across at least two intervention cycles to determine the difference between the student's baseline performance and postintervention performance. If student progress is assessed at a level consistent with predetermined goals, then the discussion may be on how best to maintain the plan over time. As noted previously, revisions might involve some streamlining of intervention components or additional assistance or accommodations. In addition, a decision may be made to fade the intervention altogether if performance gains may be maintained without individualized strategies. If there is little progress despite several well-implemented and empirically supported interventions, then more intensive intervention options might be considered. These may include psychological testing, referral to the school's committee on special education, or other types of diagnostic assessment based on the nature of the student's difficulties.

Case Example

The following case example illustrates the program evaluation phase of the FBA process as it applied to Lori, a six-year-old female student receiving special education services. This child, diagnosed previously with Down's Syndrome and autism spectrum disorder, was initially referred for "flopping" behaviors. The educators working with Lori and her parent indicated that Lori was friendly and affectionate when engaged in preferred tasks. It was also noted, however, that she flopped to the floor and rolled back and forth when she was required to transition to another task or when a demand or request was made of her. Over six days of baseline observation, Lori displayed flopping from 2 to 13 times. These incidents typically were predicted by or in response to a transition, a demand/request, or both. Given these predictors, the hypothesized function of Lori's behavior was to escape/avoid an activity or demand (transitions and requests). The average number of flopping behaviors during the baseline period was seven per day.

The intervention designed for Lori involved the use of a structured transition procedure, including both preventative and consequent procedures. Preventative procedures included the presentation of preferred items and activities (yarn, shoelaces, singing, and manipulatives) during transition times. These preferred items were removed when Lori exhibited flopping behavior and offered again for the desired transitioning behavior. In addition, when Lori flopped to the floor, the educational team engaged in a consistent procedure, including specific verbal prompts, restatement of behavioral expectations, picture cues, and removal of preferred items. The goal for the intervention was to reduce flopping by 50 percent to reduce the average number of incidents from 7 to 3.5 or fewer per day within two to three weeks.

This intervention (Intervention 1) was implemented with Lori and monitored for six school days. The team then met to review integrity data and Lori's progress graph. Given that the intervention was being implemented as designed, the team revised the intervention based on Lori's response (formative assessment). Because Lori demonstrated some progress but had not yet reached the predetermined goals, the intervention was revised (Intervention 2) by emphasizing additional preventative measures. These measures included the presentation of more recently preferred items and singing, to promote positive behavior during transition times, and a continuation of consequent procedures for flopping. These procedures were implemented for an additional six school days.

Results of the intervention are illustrated by the graph in Figure 7.3. As indicated, the mean number of flops per day during the baseline period was 7. Following the implementation of Intervention 1, Lori's flopping behavior was reduced to an average of 4.5 per day. Intervention 2 was then implemented, with additional emphasis on preventative procedures. Based on six days of monitoring Lori's behavior, flopping behavior was reduced to an average of 3.4 per day. This summative assessment indicated that the educational team was successful in reducing Lori's flopping behavior by over 50 percent. The team decided to continue the designed intervention for the remainder of the school year and

FIGURE 7.3

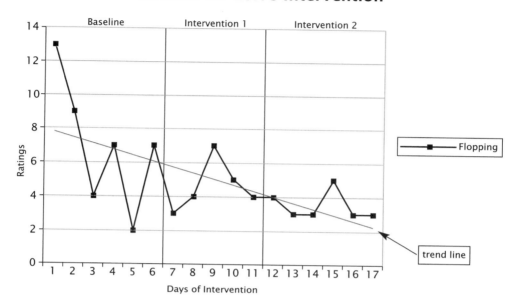

Results for Lori's Intervention

successfully reduced Lorie's flopping behavior while also improving her ability to transition through her school schedule.

Putting It All Together

In this chapter, we have reviewed the evaluation stage of the behavior intervention planning process. This final stage of the process calls for the assessment of intervention integrity, the collection and graphing of progress monitoring information, the use of this information to revise the intervention formatively, and the assessment of the overall effectiveness of the plan, or summative assessment. To illustrate the process, we also provided case examples for actual students. In the remaining chapters of the book, we will explore specific intervention ideas to assist in classroom management and to address functions of behavior commonly seen in school settings.

Intervention Plan Evaluation Checklist

Student _____ Date _____ Teacher _____

Step 1: Assess intervention integrity

❏ Can the teacher live with the plan? If yes, proceed; if no, revise the plan to improve feasibility.

❏ Can the intervention be implemented as designed? If yes, proceed. If no, decide on ways to increase integrity (e.g., additional resources, schedule changes, revision of intervention components, development of new intervention).

Step 2: Collect data and graph student progress

Create a graph including baseline data and results of student progress monitoring over each phase of the intervention.

Step 3: Conduct formative assessment

Compare student progress with baseline ratings and behavior goals. How closely did the student come to meeting the goals? *(Check appropriate outcome.)*

❏ **Exceeded or met goals:**

Maintain, streamline, or fade intervention procedures.

❏ **Showed progress/nearly met goals:**

Modify goals. (Are they too high?)

Increase the frequency or appeal of incentives.

Change the intervention vehicle (how the intervention is delivered—e.g., an incentive may be delivered by a preferred adult).

Add a new intervention component (e.g., add a consequence for negative behavior to a marginally effective incentive-based plan).

❏ **No improvement:**

Consider significant revision, or design a new intervention.

Ensure that intervention integrity has been high. Recheck FBA information (e.g., Conduct classroom observation. Was the correct function selected?)

Step 4: Conduct summative assessment

Over several cycles in the formative assessment process, did the intervention ultimately work? *(Check one.)*

❏ **Adequate improvement:**

Consider long-term implementation of the plan (maintenance) with periodic updates, or fading the intervention altogether, to see if performance gains continue.

❏ **No improvement:**

Consider more intense intervention options.

From *Functional Behavioral Assessment and Intervention in Schools: A Practitioner's Guide (Grades 1–8)*, by J. L. McDougal, S. M. Chafouleas, and B. Waterman, 2006, Champaign, IL: Research Press (800-519-2707; www.researchpress.com)

Daily Behavior Intervention Checklist

Student _____ Date _____

Teacher/Observer _____

Intervention(s) _____

_____

List each step of the intervention(s). If necessary, add extra spaces. Circle the rating for each step.

1 = I completed this step today.

2 = I partially completed this step today.

3 = I did not complete this step today.

Intervention steps   *Rating scale*

1. _____   1   2   3

_____

2. _____   1   2   3

_____

3. _____   1   2   3

_____

4. _____   1   2   3

_____

5. _____   1   2   3

_____

6. _____   1   2   3

_____

7. _____   1   2   3

_____

Comments

_____

_____

_____

From *Functional Behavioral Assessment and Intervention in Schools: A Practitioner's Guide (Grades 1–8)*, by J. L. McDougal, S. M. Chafouleas, and B. Waterman, 2006, Champaign, IL: Research Press (800-519-2707; www.researchpress.com)

CHAPTER 8

Interventions to Promote Skill Development

In this chapter, we shift the focus from describing the assessment and intervention process to providing actual scripts for intervention. This chapter and the two subsequent chapters present interventions designed to be effective and feasible in the school setting (e.g., McDougal & Clonan, 2002). Best-practice considerations include focusing on important and socially valid behaviors; employing procedures with empirical support; employing procedures that are simple to use, generally positive in nature, believed to be effective, and well-matched to the school environment; and using intervention scripts to facilitate reliable implementation (Telzrow & Beebe, 2002). To facilitate proper implementation, performance feedback and technical assistance should be given to educators, and periodic integrity checks should be made to assess the extent to which the intervention is being implemented as designed (McDougal, Clonan, & Martens, 2000).

We agree with Tilly and Flugum (1995) that an intervention represents a planned modification to the environment designed to alter behavior in a specific and predetermined fashion. An intervention also represents a set of strategies and procedures to improve a student's performance and decrease the difference between the student's behavior and what is expected in the school environment (Upah & Tilly, 2002). In keeping with these considerations, the interventions described here are environmental modifications designed to improve student performance with clearly specified, goal-directed plans.

Why Skill-Based Interventions Are Needed

As discussed previously, problem behaviors are sometimes related to academic or behavioral skill deficits or communicative intent. Some children simply do not have the skills necessary to engage in the required academic, social, or communicative behaviors. The direct teaching of such skills, then, is essential because a child must first have the skill before being able to apply it. The skill-building interventions described in the following paragraphs are based on general principles of good teaching, including modeling, feedback and practice, and structured opportunities to generalize the new skills across situations and settings. These intervention ideas should be noted in the teaching and support section of the Assessment-to-Intervention Worksheet (included as Figure 6.2) when FBA information suggests the presence of a skill-based deficit.

This chapter describes interventions that are designed to improve behavioral skills, academic skills, and communication skills. Some are designed for use with individual students; others may be implemented at the group, class, or schoolwide level. Each strategy is described briefly, and guidelines for use are given. In addition, each strategy is accompanied by a brief key that provides handy information on appropriate ages, estimated time for implementation, and required materials. The interventions described here are not intended as an exhaustive list. Instead, this is a brief guide to some effective skill-building strategies. Also provided are references to more detailed works.

The following reproducible forms are provided at the end of this chapter:

> Worksheet 8.1: Behavior Matrix
>
> Worksheet 8.2: Survivor Skills Worksheet
>
> Worksheet 8.3: Targeted Skills Worksheet
>
> Worksheet 8.4: Functional Communication Training Worksheet

Interventions to Build Behavioral Skills

Students are most likely to demonstrate skill deficits when behavioral expectations are unclear, infrequently practiced or reinforced, or inconsistently monitored. Often students develop the necessary "school skills" by following the rules, routines, and structure of the school or classroom and by meeting those expectations. Therefore, to be most effective, behavior skill training should begin at the start of the school year. Behaviors also need to be modeled, practiced, and reinforced, as well as generalized across settings and time. Ideally, these skills should be taught to all students, in the building and in the classrooms, across settings, and over time.

The Behavior Matrix is offered as one approach for organizing comprehensive behavior skills training in the school setting. For additional information on schoolwide approaches to teaching and promoting positive behavior, readers may visit the Web sites of the National Positive Behavior Intervention and Support (PBIS) Center (http:// www.pbis.org) and the PBIS training headquarters (http://www.ebdnetwork-il.org).*

Even when well-implemented schoolwide programs exist, specific classrooms, student groups, or individual students may require additional instruction. Therefore, the other two intervention tools described here—the Survivor Skills and Targeted Skills procedures—are appropriate for classwide, group, and individual use. In summary, the following three tools are presented in this section:

> *Behavior Matrix.* This procedure and corresponding worksheet document the behavioral expectations in a school or classroom and break each of those expectations into component skills. It then serves as a template whereby the necessary skills can be taught to students in each of the required settings.

---

*Many of the ideas for the behavior skill training materials that follow have been adapted from unpublished training materials developed by the Illinois PBIS coordinators, coaches and school teams, and the Office of Special Education's National PBIS Center. Special thanks to Lucille Eber and Steven Romano for their training assistance.

Survivor Skills. This procedure and worksheet offer a lesson planner for educators to develop skill instruction for specific problematic behaviors (e.g., running in the hall, calling out in class). These lessons are usually delivered to an entire class or grade-level team of classrooms where a high number of similar types of misbehavior have been noted. They may also be implemented in challenging settings such as the cafeteria or playground.

Targeted Skills. This procedure and worksheet help educators to develop targeted and individualized social skills instruction for a specific student or a small group of students with similar needs. The procedure may be used to teach specific skills in areas such as anger management or conflict resolution. A number of well-established social skills programs exist. Educators may want to adopt one of these programs to guide behavioral skill instruction. Among the better known programs are *Skillstreaming* (Goldstein & McGinnis, 1997; McGinnis & Goldstein, 1997); and the *Stop and Think Social Skills Training Program* (Knoff, 2002). Among the many skills they teach are beginning a conversation, following instructions, identifying feelings, asking for help, dealing with anger, making a complaint, and saying no.

Behavior Matrix

Grades: K–8

Time: 2–3 hours

Materials: Behavior Matrix Worksheet; posterboard and markers

This tool comes from the Positive Behavior Intervention and Support (PBIS) model and is well-suited to guide behavioral skill training throughout the school and in individual classrooms. In the PBIS model, a school-based team meets regularly to develop three to five consistent expectations (e.g., be responsible, be respectful, be prepared). They use the matrix to describe the specific component skills that are required for each expectation across each setting in which the skills are typically encountered. These expectations and component skills are then posted around the building and used by educators to guide direct instruction of the expected behaviors.

A sample Behavior Matrix Worksheet is given as Figure 8.1; a blank version of this form appears at the end of this chapter.

Procedure

1. *Choose three to five positive expectations for schoolwide implementation.* First, convene a schoolwide planning team. Then identify expectations that can be consistently applied throughout the school. List these expectations on the left-hand side of the matrix form, one expectation per box.

2. *Identify the predominant school settings in which students will display these skills.* List these settings on the horizontal boxes on the top of the form.

FIGURE 8.1

Sample Behavior Matrix Worksheet

Settings → Expectations	Classroom	Hall	Playground	Cafeteria	Dismissal/Arrival	Bathroom
Be respectful	Raise hand Respect others' property Listen while others are speaking	Quiet voices Quiet feet Respect personal space	Use proper language Respect equipment Share equipment	Quiet voices Wait your turn Follow adult directions	Quiet voices Quiet feet Respect personal space Follow all directions	Knock on stall Give others privacy Use quiet voices
Be here and be ready	Try your best Be on time Have supplies ready Do quality work	Walk single file Face front Use hall pass	Stop on signal Walk to and from the playground	Wait at table for signal Know lunch Line up on signal	Observe quiet time during morning announcements number prior to dismissal Follow arrival procedures Follow dismissal procedures	Use bathroom pass Return to class when finished Observe quiet time
Be safe	Walk Hands and feet to self Feet and chairs on floor Be a problem solver	Hands at side Walk	Follow adult direction No play fighting Follow rules of playground	Walk to line Stay in seat Sit with feet on floor, bottom on chair, facing table Food on tray	Walk Hands at sides	Wash hands with soap and water Feet on floor Throw towels in garbage
Be caring	Use kind words Be a good friend Help others Share Be truthful	Look, don't touch	Use kind words	Be polite and actions	Greet others Say please and thank you	Flush toilet Say hello and goodbye Use kind words

From *Functional Behavioral Assessment and Intervention in Schools: A Practitioner's Guide (Grades 1–8)*, by J. L. McDougal, S. M. Chafouleas, and B. Waterman, 2006, Champaign, IL: Research Press (800-519-2707; www.researchpress.com)

3. *Identify component skills.* For each expectation, identify the skills needed to be successful in each setting. List these skills in the appropriate space on the form. For example, to be respectful in the hallways students might need to use their inside voices, walk to the right, and keep their hands to themselves.

4. *Begin on the first day of school.* After the matrix has been developed and approved for use, behavioral skill instruction begins. Ideally, it begins on the first day of school, when teachers transition their classes among instructional stations set up in a variety of settings, such as the hallway, cafeteria, and classroom. At each station, students learn the expected behavior for that setting and are given both examples (e.g., students walking in the hallway) and "nonexamples" (e.g., students running in the hallway) of the behavior.

5. *Post and patrol.* These expectations should be posted throughout the school, and the behaviors should be monitored by all adults in the building. Precorrection procedures are encouraged (e.g., teachers review hallway expectations prior to dismissal), and adults agree to be consistent in correcting student behavior (e.g., students caught running in the hall are required to go back and walk).

IMPLEMENTATION TIPS

To make the behavior matrix more effective, consider the following ideas:

- *Reward positive behavior.* Positive behaviors may be increased by implementing schoolwide and classwide recognition and incentive systems. For example, a school might implement a "gotcha being good" program, where staff randomly reinforce students' positive behavior with "gotcha" tickets that may be collected and redeemed for small prizes.

- *Give "booster shots."* Activities on the first day of school should be reinforced throughout the year through booster sessions and a variety of schoolwide as well as classroom-based incentive programs. Additional instruction may be provided for commonly occurring infractions (e.g., running and pushing in the hall) or to assist particular students (e.g., any student referred to the office more than once per academic quarter).

- *Evaluate progress.* Office referral information and teacher reports can help educators and school teams identify skills and settings in need of remediation. These sources of information also should be used to monitor progress (e.g., decline in bus referral, fewer teacher reports of chaotic cafeteria behavior).

- *Celebrate success.* As often as possible, celebrate success. Students and classes caught being great might be mentioned in the morning announcements, for example. In addition, identified behavioral improvements can be shared during faculty meetings, and positive notes may be sent home to promote and communicate success.

Survivor Skills

Grades: K–8

Time: 1 hour

Materials: Survivor Skills Worksheet

This procedure is helpful in designing lessons to teach the "whole island" of students specific behavioral skills to survive in school. Skill instruction with the Survivor Skills Worksheet is generally conducted with an entire class (or even several classrooms on a given team) when there is a commonly occurring problem (e.g., frequent call-outs) or anticipated difficulties (e.g., prior to a field trip).

Figure 8.2 shows a sample Survivor Skills Worksheet; a blank version appears at the end of the chapter.

Procedure

1. *Teach the expected behaviors.* This generally involves the following steps:

   Provide a clear expectation (posted prominently in the classroom).

   Define component skills (how students meet the expectation).

   Teach across settings (or in a targeted setting).

2. *Model expected behaviors.* Provide examples and nonexamples (e.g., demonstrate inside voice as well as voice level that is too loud for use inside the school). Have students role-play and model both behavioral examples and nonexamples.

3. *Practice and reinforce expected behaviors.* Look out for and praise positive behavior when you notice it. Also consider implementing an incentive-based system to reinforce positive behavior further. Implement precorrection strategies (review expected behavior prior to beginning the task or entering the setting), design error correction strategies (e.g., students must go back and walk the hall if they run) and make use of guided practice procedures (e.g., practice dismissal procedures prior to the end of the day).

4. *Modify the setting to limit potential for negative behavior.* Consider decreasing transition time, using physical cues (e.g., turn lights off for quiet), pairing students of different abilities, and rearranging seating. Generally think of new ways to design the classroom to support success.

5. *Generalize skills across settings and times.* Design opportunities to practice skills across settings in which problematic behavior occurs. Provide additional training both in problematic settings (e.g., hallways) and in preparation for difficult times of the year (e.g., just before the winter holiday break, before the arrival of a substitute teacher).

6. *Repeat this process as necessary.*

FIGURE 8.2

Sample Survivor Skills Worksheet

Teacher ___Mrs. Washington___ Date ___2/7/07___

Step 1: Teaching

Expectation: _Responsible hallway behavior_

Necessary skills: _Quiet, hands at side, single file, stay to the right_

Relevant settings: _Arrival, dismissal, transitions to/from special classes_

Step 2: Modeling

List examples: _Teacher will model each skill in the hall; students will role-play._

List nonexamples: _Teacher will model a nonexample of each skill in the hall; students will role-play._

Describe role-plays: _After teacher modeling, selected students will be asked to perform both expected skills and nonexamples of each skill, while the class watches. Students will be asked why each skill is necessary and important._

Step 3: Practicing and reinforcing

How and where will practice occur? _This week, prior to each hall transition, the teacher will remind students of expected behaviors. As correction, the class will go back and walk properly any section of hall not correctly transitioned._

How and where will reinforcement occur? _Teacher praise and random reinforcers (e.g., small snack, extra free time) will be used to promote responsible hall behavior._

Step 4: Modifying the setting

List setting modifications: _The teacher will turn off the lights to signal a transition and then line students up alphabetically. The class will proceed only when quiet and in single file._

Step 5. Generalizing for success

Across which settings and times? _During hallway transitions, especially during arrival, dismissal, and special times._

How will training occur? _See practice and reinforcement procedures._

IMPLEMENTATION TIPS

To make survivor skills instruction more effective, consider the following ideas:

- *Link survivor skills to building-wide expectations.* Each skill taught can be linked to a building-wide expectation, especially if the behavior matrix procedures are implemented in the building from the beginning of the year.
- *Reward positive behavior.* Recognize, praise, and reward (e.g., with a lottery ticket) desired behavior to promote it in the classroom.
- *Let students participate.* During teaching, consider using a tell, show, do, and reflect format. After telling and showing students the desired behavior, design activities in which students engage in the behavior and have a chance to reflect on it.

Targeted Skills

Grades: K–8

Time: 2 hours and up

Materials: Targeted Skills Worksheet

Even when clear behavioral expectations are taught, practiced, and reinforced, some individuals and small groups of students may require additional social skills instruction—for example, in anger management or conflict resolution. This format is one approach to designing and implementing social skills instruction. The series of steps to teach social skills to individuals or small groups has been presented by others (see Witt, Daly, & Noell, 2000); the technique consists of skill teaching, modeling, practicing and reinforcing, and generalizing. This technique can be applied to the teaching of social, anger management, and conflict resolution skills because it provides a foundation for skill instruction, particularly at a small-group level. The steps in this process are quite similar to those described in the preceding survivor skills section and so will not be further described here.

A sample Targeted Skills Worksheet for Marie appears as Figure 8.3. A blank version appears as Worksheet 8.3, at the end of the chapter.

Procedure

The targeted skills approach is illustrated by the case of Julie, a seventh grader who has had a long-lasting problem with another girl, Marie, in her class. They have had several loud verbal arguments, and on one occasion engaged in a physical fight. Julie is targeted as a student who may benefit from skill teaching in the area of conflict resolution. Although several skill deficits in this area are suspected, the teacher and school psychologist decide to work with both Julie and Marie on negotiation skills.

A plan to monitor Julie's and Marie's behavior across settings was developed, and both have been allowed to select an incentive at the end of each conflict-free week. The girls are allowed to visit the school psychologist's office periodically to

FIGURE 8.3

Sample Targeted Skills Worksheet

Student(s) _Julie, Marie, others_   Date _3/9/06_

Teacher _Mr. Helmick_

Type of skill to be taught:

❑ Survival (e.g., listening, following directions, ignoring distractions)

❑ Interpersonal (e.g., sharing, asking permission, learning how to interrupt)

❑ Problem solving (e.g., asking for help, apologizing, setting a goal)

❑ Anger management (e.g., identifying triggers and reducers)

☑ Conflict resolution (e.g., recognizing conflict, negotiation, mediation)

Step 1: Select the behavior and develop a teaching plan.

The behaviors to be taught are in the area of conflict resolution—specifically, recognizing when conflict exists, communicating effectively and honestly, identifying the perspective of others, identifying areas of agreement, and formalizing an agreement. These skills will be taught in a small-group setting over the course of six weeks.

Considerations:

Have the student(s) ever demonstrated the desired skill? If so, in what situations?

No. These students tend to move to an "all or nothing" position very quickly when confronted with conflict.

Does cuing help? If so, consider teaching self-monitoring techniques.

No. Typically, by the time an adult intercedes, emotions have become too energized for cuing to have much impact on behavior.

How do socially competent peers gain the positive consequence or outcome?

The subskills that socially competent peers demonstrate include the ability to clearly articulate their wants, needs, and feelings; express their positions and interests; take the perspective of others; generate possible solutions; and jointly agree upon a solution.

What strengths do the student(s) bring to the learning process?

Step 2: Select students who will participate in the group.

I have nominated four students in addition to Julie and Marie to participate in weekly groups: Randall, Maya, Burton, and Min.

Considerations:

Include both high-status and low-status peers.

Begin with team-building exercises (e.g., naming the group and drawing a picture that illustrates it).

Include some children who are competent in the skill and others who are not.

Step 3: What is the rationale for teaching and using the skill?

Considerations:

Explain the positive outcomes that will be gained and the negatives avoided.

Conflict negotiation and resolution are important interpersonal skills for success in school and beyond.

FIGURE 8.3 (continued)

Ensure that the students know the skill and can give a rationale for applying it.

Julie, Marie, and the group will discuss the negative responses to conflict (e.g., potential for violence, incarceration, and war) and positive consequences that have occurred as a result of positively negotiated conflict (e.g., civil rights).

Step 4: Indicate plan to model the desired behavior (by teacher and competent peers).

We will identify Dr. Martin Luther King, Gandhi, and Rosa Parks as great individuals who responded to conflict in productive ways. We will also identify two situations in our own lives where we responded to conflict in a productive way. We will encourage group members to share similar experiences.

Step 5: How will guided practice occur?

Considerations:

Use prompts, guided feedback, and role-play situations.

Fade prompts when students become proficient.

Break skills into smaller components when necessary.

Group members will act out appropriate responses to a variety of conflict situations until each student can demonstrate the skills with limited feedback from others. When Julie and Marie next have a confrontation, they will be guided through the use of listening and sharing skills, generating solutions to the problem, and jointly selecting a solution.

Step 6: Develop a plan for independent practice.

Considerations:

Find ways to reinforce independent skill use.

Identify positive natural consequences for engaging in the skill.

When Julie experiences a conflict with another student, I will encourage her to identify and implement one of the skills from the group. After calming down, Julie will tell the other student why she was upset and attempt to settle the dispute peacefully.

If these students are unable to independently listen to the others' concerns, share their own, or develop solutions, I will increase my prompting and feedback, and refer the situation back to the group to process there.

Step 7: Develop a plan to practice in multiple settings.

Considerations:

Where can the student(s) perform the skill in new but similar settings?

How can the behavior be reinforced?

Can the student(s) consistently perform the targeted skill across situations and with different individuals?

Provide prompts and guided practice as needed.

Julie and Marie's behavior will be monitored across multiple settings (classroom, cafeteria, specials), and each student will be allowed to select an incentive at the end of every conflict-free week. They may also visit the school psychologist's office periodically to discuss progress and situations they find challenging. The art and music teachers will give Julie positive prompting and feedback when appropriate.

discuss their progress as well as any situations that they find challenging to negotiate peacefully. In addition, the art and music teachers were asked to give both girls positive prompting and feedback when appropriate.

The preceding example illustrates that conflict in both home and school environments is unavoidable but can be positive when it leads to greater understanding, increased commitment, or improved decision making. Unfortunately, lack of conflict resolution skills may mean that a conflict ends in name-calling, threats, or physical aggression. Other skills that may help promote positive interpersonal interactions include the following:

Communication skills

Finding alternatives to violence

Problem-solving skills

Learning appropriate ways to express anger

Setting achievable goals

Using self-monitoring techniques

Interventions to Build Academic Skills

As discussed previously, interventions for academic skill deficits should focus on the appropriate step in the instructional hierarchy; in other words, interventions should be designed to promote accuracy, fluency, and generalization. In addition, specific reasons for the difficulty (task too hard, needs more practice, needs more assistance, needs to generalize skill, etc.) should be considered. Thus decisions about interventions for academic skill deficits require multiple considerations, with the goal of conducting a task analysis of the specific skill to be taught. This portion of the chapter will present general intervention strategies for each of the skill-based reasons for academic difficulty. Table 8.1 summarizes the academic interventions, arranged by reason for the academic difficulty and stage in the instructional hierarchy addressed by each intervention. The following discussion provides examples and intervention protocols that educators may use to design and guide implementation of individualized academic interventions.

Is the task too hard for the student?
If yes, consider these options.

Slice back the skill. This strategy is appropriate when a student can perform some but not all of a skill. The goal in "slicing back" is to modify the skill to decrease the number of required steps. Thus the procedure is to divide the task into smaller parts, increasing the required steps over time as the student demonstrates mastery. Examples include using graphic organizers and paragraph organizers to assist students with writing tasks, use of structured worksheets to guide students through division calculation, and use of controlled vocabulary in books for beginning readers.

TABLE 8.1

Academic Interventions by Reason for Difficulty and Stage of the Instructional Hierarchy

Reason for Academic Difficulty	Intervention Strategy	Instructional Stage
• Work is too hard.	Slice back the skill Step back the skill	Accuracy
• Needs more practice.	Listening passage preview Mad-minute math	Fluency
• Needs more assistance.	Listening passage preview Repeated reading Say it and move it	Accuracy
• Needs more practice and help.	Error correction: cover-copy-compare, phrase drill for reading, paired reading	Accuracy
	Performance feedback (response cards, story retelling)	Accuracy and fluency
• Needs to generalize skill.	Applied tasks Recognition tasks	Generalization

Step back the skill. This intervention is appropriate for the student who is not performing any aspect of the skill correctly. The goal in "stepping back" is to teach an easier skill or use less difficult materials. An example is moving to a lower level book for a frustrated reader, reteaching addition facts prior to multiplication, and reteaching outlining and the components of a paragraph prior to an essay assignment.

> *Note: These intervention suggestions can be found in Wolery, Bailey, and Sugai (1988).*

Does the student need more practice?

If yes, then consider drill and practice techniques such as the following.

Repeated reading. This intervention provides the opportunity for the student to practice the same material repeatedly. The steps are as follows:

1. Select the passage to be used in the intervention.

2. Tell the student you will be monitoring how long it takes him or her to read the passage.

3. Have the student read the passage while elapsed time is recorded. If the student hesitates for three seconds, pronounce the word for the student.

4. After finishing, tell the student how long it took to read the passage.

5. Repeat these steps two or three more times so that the student has read the entire passage three to four times total.

Mad-minute math. This intervention provides the opportunity to practice under timed conditions, reinforcing accurate and fast performance. The steps are as follows:

1. Select the task to accomplish, such as a worksheet containing math computation problems.

2. Tell the student that he or she will have x minutes to answer as many problems as quickly as possible.

3. Monitor the time, telling the student to stop when the allotted time has elapsed. Correct the student's answers.

4. Provide feedback on performance. Remind students who rush and make mistakes that the goal is to answer both correctly and quickly.

Does the student need more assistance?

If so, consider the level of help needed and select an intervention such as the following.

MODELING INTERVENTIONS
(APPROPRIATE FOR BUILDING ACCURACY)

Listening passage preview/repeated reading. In this intervention, the instructor first models accurate reading, then has the student practice reading the same material while the instructor monitors performance. The steps are as follows:

1. Select the passage to be used in the intervention.

2. Read the entire passage to the student at a rate between 120 and 140 words per minute. Have the student follow along on a student copy.

3. Tell the student you will be monitoring how long it takes him or her to read the passage.

4. Have the student read the passage while elapsed time is recorded. If the student hesitates for three seconds, say the word for the student.

5. After finishing, tell the student how long it took to read the passage.

6. Repeat the procedures one to two more times so that the student is exposed to the entire passage three to four times total.

Say it and move it. This intervention teaches letter-sound correspondences using manipulatives. "Say it and move it" sheets must be prepared ahead of time. They have blank boxes corresponding to the number of sounds in a word to be taught (words with two, three, or four sounds). Students are then given manipulatives (e.g., checkers or, later, plastic letters) to move into a box as each sound is pronounced. Steps are as follows:

1. Provide the student with the worksheet and manipulatives.

2. Tell the student to watch you as you say a word.

3. As each sound in the word is slowly pronounced, move one manipulative into a box (moving from left to right).

4. When all sounds are completed, repeat the entire word, moving your finger from left to right across the boxes.

5. Have the student repeat the word.

6. Remove the manipulatives, and have the student "say it and move it."

Note: More detail about this intervention can be found in Blachman, Ball, Black, and Tangel (2000).

ERROR CORRECTION INTERVENTIONS
(APPROPRIATE FOR BUILDING ACCURACY)

Cover-copy-compare for spelling. In this intervention, students independently study, attempt correct spelling, and then check performance. This technique also can be used with math computation and vocabulary. Steps are as follows:

1. Prepare the list of words to be spelled, writing down a column on the left-hand side of a page.

2. Provide the list to the student to study.

3. Instruct the student to cover the column. One word at a time, the student then uncovers the word to study it.

4. Next the student covers the word and writes it in the right-hand column.

5. Finally, the student uncovers the word in the left-hand column and compares what he or she has written with the correct spelling. Incorrectly spelled words should be corrected and practiced three times.

Phrase drill for reading. This strategy involves having the student correctly repeat the phrase surrounding an incorrectly read word. Steps are as follows:

1. Choose an appropriate reading selection.

2. Tell the student to begin reading out loud and that you will help him or her read words that are unknown.

3. If the student makes a mistake or encounters an unknown word, pronounce the correct word.

4. Read the entire phrase surrounding that word while the student follows along by pointing with his finger.

5. Have the student repeat the correct phrase or sentence.

6. Continue having the student read the passage.

Incorrectly read words can be placed on index cards. The cards can be repeatedly shuffled and practiced until the words written on them are mastered.

Note: See http://www.interventioncentral.com for more information.

Paired reading. In this intervention, a student reads aloud with an experienced reader. This strategy works well when implemented with peer tutoring. Steps are as follows:

1. Select appropriate reading material.

2. Seat the student and experienced reader so that both can view the selection.

3. State that the experienced reader will read aloud along with the student.

4. Instruct the student to provide a signal (e.g., hand tap) when he or she wants to read aloud alone.

5. If the student encounters an unknown word (either misread or unread), the experienced reader is to point to the word, state it, and have the student repeat it.

6. The experienced reader continues to read along with the student until the student signals again.

Note: More information on this intervention can be found in Topping (1987).

PERFORMANCE FEEDBACK INTERVENTIONS
(APPROPRIATE FOR BUILDING ACCURACY AND FLUENCY)

Response cards or choral tasks. These interventions are usually used as group-response techniques to engage students in the material being taught. Any content questions that can be answered in short responses (one to three words) are appropriate. Steps are as follows:

1. Select the material and a cue to signal student response. If using response cards, then provide blank cards to write on or yes/no cards to the students to hold up when responding.

2. Teach the cue to the students through modeling and practice. If using choral responding, make sure to demonstrate the appropriate voice level for responding.

3. Keeping an appropriately motivating pace, provide the question and then pause before giving the cue to respond.

4. If incorrect answers are offered, provide immediate feedback on the correct response to the entire group rather than singling out an individual.

5. Consider presenting incorrectly answered items again later in the lesson.

Note: More information about this technique can be found at http://www.interventioncentral.com.

Story retelling for reading comprehension. This intervention gives students the opportunity to organize the information they read and receive feedback on the accuracy of their recall of the story. Steps are as follows:

1. Select appropriate reading material. Create a story outline that includes key points to consider, such as writing down the first, second, and third important ideas with detail to support the ideas.

2. Have students work in pairs or individually with an adult.

3. Tell students they will be asked to read the material silently and pick out the important ideas.

4. Review the story outline with the students, modeling how to complete it and practicing with examples.

5. Have students read the story and complete the outline.

6. Have students take turns to retell the important story ideas to a peer or an adult. If using peers, collect the outlines and use them to monitor progress and provide feedback to each student. Feedback should not involve correction on responses; all responses should be considered correct.

Note: More information on story retelling can be found in Gambrell, Pfeiffer, and Wilson (1985).

Does the student need to generalize the skills?

If so, consider the following techniques.

Design an applied task. Design a task that requires the student to use the acquired skills in a setting outside of the normal classroom or assignment. For example, have students read and discuss newspaper articles, write to county legislators, or compute sales tax on a list of acquired goods.

Promote recognition of when to apply the skill. Another generalization strategy is to arrange problems so that students have to apply the correct operation or procedure. For example, students may read sight words in text, give mixed calculation or word problems in math, and circle capitalization errors in a writing sample designed to contain such errors.

An Intervention to Build Communication Skills: Functional Communication Training

The final skill deficit addressed in this chapter is communication. When a child with challenging behavior also has expressive language delays, and especially when that child is diagnosed with a developmental delay or disorder (e.g., autism), the communicative intent of this behavior must be assessed. Functional communication training (FCT) is a procedure to develop and teach adaptive communicative responses to individuals who have limited expressive repertoires so that their needs will be met and their challenging behavior reduced. This intervention is usually conducted by a multidisciplinary team, potentially composed of teachers, speech and language therapists, psychologists, and other educators working with the child.

Grades: K–8

Time: Varies widely

Materials: Functional Communication Training Worksheet; communication symbols

The procedure usually involves identifying the student's need or desire; designing an appropriate and feasible communication cue; teaching, modeling, and reinforcing its use; and ensuring that the challenging behavior is no longer functional. As a result, FCT is usually done in the context of an individualized functional assessment and intervention plan.

Figure 8.4 offers a sample Functional Communication Training Worksheet; a blank version appears at the end of the chapter.

Procedure

1. *Teach the child.* Teach specific phrases, cues, symbols, or pictures to address each of the areas identified in the assessment stage (e.g., solicit adult attention, request assistance, request a break from task).

2. *Model the expected communication behaviors.* Provide examples throughout the day and prompt the student to use the new form of communication.

3. *Practice and reinforce the functional communication.* Provide structured training sessions, differentially reinforce use of the communication system (e.g., with praise, task assistance, a break), and over time increase use throughout the day. Ensure that negative behavior is no longer functional (it is not reinforced).

4. *Structure the setting.* Training is usually conducted initially in a small, well-controlled setting with limited distractions. The training sessions should be regulated in duration, time of day, and location.

5. *Generalize use of the communication system.* After the student becomes proficient with the skills in a structured setting, the skills can be generalized for use in less controlled environments and with other individuals in the building.

See the chapter references for a list of works containing more detailed information on FCT.

IMPLEMENTATION TIPS

To make FCT instruction most effective, consider the following:

- *Ensure efficiency of new communication form.* Make sure that the communication form is more efficient and effective for the student than the challenging behavior. The ease with which the student can perform the task and the interpretability of the message are important considerations.

- *Use popular communication systems.* Two popular communication systems for nonverbal individuals are the Picture Exchange Communication System (PECS) and American Sign Language (ASL). Popular symbols include the Mayer-Johnson Picture Communication symbols and the computer program Boardmaker (http://www.mayerjohnson.com).

FIGURE 8.4

Sample Functional Communication Training Worksheet

Student _____*Todd*_____ Date _____*1/18/06*_____

Step 1: Teach

Symbol/cue/phrase: *Point to a break symbol on a desk.*

Student need/desire: *To signal fatigue and need for a brief break.*

Step 2: Model

Who will model expected communication? *The speech and language therapist.*

How will the student be prompted? *By pointing to the break symbol and asking Todd if he needs a break.*

Describe the modeling plan. *During speech and language time, when Todd becomes disruptive and appears fatigued, he will be prompted to point to the break symbol.*

Step 3: Practice and reinforce

How and where will practice occur? *During individual speech and language therapy times.*

How and where will reinforcement occur? *Todd will be provided with a two-minute break each time he points to the break symbol. If breaks become too frequent, the teacher will consider providing a preferred incentive and two-minute break for each 10 consecutive minutes Todd remains on task.*

How will negative (target) behavior be addressed? *Disruptive behavior will be ignored, and prompts for taking a break will be provided.*

Step 4: Structure the setting

Where will formal training occur (location, duration, time of day)? *In the speech and language room for a half-hour per day, at Todd's regular afternoon time.*

Step 5: Generalize for success

Across which settings and times? *After three training sessions, the paraprofessional working with Todd in the classroom will begin to implement the plan throughout the school day.*

How will training occur? *The speech and language therapist will provide training and half-hour twice-weekly performance feedback sessions to the paraprofessional for two weeks.*

Selected Resources

General Interventions

Telzrow, C. F., & Beebe, J. J. (2002). Best practices in facilitating intervention adherence and integrity. In A. Thomas & J. Grimes (Eds.), *Best practices in school psychology* (4th ed.; pp. 483–501). Bethesda, MD: National Association of School Psychologists.

Tilly, W. D. III, & Flugum, K. R. (1995). Best practices in ensuring quality interventions. In A. Thomas & J. Grimes (Eds.), *Best practices in school psychology* (3rd ed.; pp. 485–500). Bethesda, MD: National Association of School Psychologists.

Upah, K. R., & Tilly, W. D. (2002). Best practices in designing, implementing, and evaluating quality interventions. In A. Thomas & J. Grimes (Eds.), *Best practices in school psychology* (4th ed., pp. 483–501). Bethesda, MD: National Association of School Psychologists.

Behavioral Interventions

Bos, C. S., & Vaughn, S. (1994). *Strategies for teaching students with learning and behavior problems.* Boston: Allyn & Bacon.

Goldstein, A., & McGinnis, E. (2001). *Skillstreaming the adolescent: New strategies and perspectives for teaching social skills.* Champaign, IL: Research Press.

Hazel, J. S., Schumaker, J. B., Sherman, J. A., & Sheldon-Wildgen, J. B. (1981). *ASSET: A social skills program for adolescents.* Champaign, IL: Research Press.

King, J. (2002). *Schoolwide social skills program.* [Online]. Available at http://www.wsdl.org/john-mking/Social_Skills.htm.

Knoff, H., & Batsche, G. M. (1995). Project ACHIEVE: Analyzing a school reform process for at-risk and underachieving students. *School Psychology Review, 24,* 579–603.

Johnson, D. W., & Johnson, R. T. (1996). Peacemakers: Teaching students to resolve their own and schoolmates' conflicts. *Focus on Exceptional Children, 28,* 1–11.

Johnson, D. W., Johnson, R. T., & Holubec, E. J. (1993). *Cooperation in the classroom* (6th ed.). Edina, MN: Interaction Books.

La Greca, A. M., & Mesibov, G. B. (1981). Facilitating interpersonal functioning with peers of learning disabled children. *Journal of Learning Disabilities, 14,* 197–199, 238.

La Greca, A. M., & Santogrossi, D. A. (1980). Social skills training: A behavioral group approach. *Journal of Consulting and Clinical Psychology, 48,* 220–228.

La Greca, A. M., Stone, W. L., & Noriega-Garcia, A. (1989). Social skills intervention: A case of a learning disabled boy. In M. C. Roberts & C. E. Walker (Eds.), *Case studies in clinical child/pediatric psychology* (pp. 139–160). New York: Guilford Press.

Witt, J. C., Daly, E. M., & Noell, G. (2000). *Functional assessments: A step-by-step guide to solving academic and behavior problems.* Longmont, CO: Sopris West.

Academic Interventions

Blachman, B. A., Ball, E. W., Black, R. S., & Tangel, D. M. (2000). *Road to the code: A phonological awareness program for young children.* Baltimore: Brookes Publishing Company.

Gambrell, L. B., Pfeiffer, W. R., & Wilson, R. M. (1985). The effects of retelling upon reading comprehension and recall of text information. *Journal of Educational Research, 78,* 216–220.

Topping, K. (1987). Paired reading: A powerful technique for parent use. *Reading Teacher, 40,* 608–614.

Witt, J. C., Daly, E. M., & Noell, G. (2000). *Functional assessments: A step-by-step guide to solving academic and behavior problems.* Longmont, CO: Sopris West.

Wolery, M., Bailey, D. B., & Sugai, G. M. (1988). *Effective teaching: Principles and procedures of applied behavior analysis with exceptional students.* Needham, MA: Allyn & Bacon.

Communicative Interventions

Carr, E. G., & Durand, V. M. (1985). Reducing behavior problems through functional communication training. *Journal of Applied Behavior Analysis, 18,* 111–126.

Carr, E. G., Levin, L., McConnachie, G., Carlson, J. I., Kemp, D. C., & Smith, C. E. (1994). *Communication-based intervention for problem behavior: A user's guide for producing positive change.* Baltimore: Paul H. Brookes.

Carr, E. G., Levin, L., McConnachie, G., Carlson, J. I., Kemp, D.C., Smith, C. E., & Magito-McLaughlin, D. (1999). Comprehensive multi-situational intervention for problem behavior in the community: Long-term maintenance and social validation. *Journal of Positive Behavior Support, 1,* 5–25.

Day, H. M., Horner, R. H., & O'Neill, R. E. (1994). Multiple functions of problem behaviors: Assessment and intervention. *Journal of Applied Behavior Analysis, 27,* 279–289.

Derby, K. M., Wacker, D. P., Berg, W., DeRaad, A., Ulrich, S., Asmus, J., Harding, J., Prouty, A., Laffey, P., & Stoner, E. A. (1997). The long-term effects of functional communication training in home settings. *Journal of Applied Behavior Analysis, 30,* 507–531.

Durand, V. M. (1990). *Severe behavior problems: A functional communication training approach.* New York: Guilford Press.

Durand, V. M., Berotti, D., & Weiner, J. S. (1993). Functional communication training: Factors affecting effectiveness, generalization, and maintenance. In J. Reichle & D. P. Wacker (Eds.), *Communicative alternatives to challenging behavior* (pp. 317–340). Baltimore: Paul H. Brookes.

Durand, V. M., & Carr, E. G. (1991). Functional communication training to reduce challenging behavior: Maintenance and application in new settings. *Journal of Applied Behavior Analysis, 24,* 251–264.

Wacker, D. P., Steege, M. W., Northup, J., Sasso, G., Berg, W., Reimers, T., Cooper, L., Cigrand, K., & Donn, L. (1990). A component analysis of functional communication training across three topographies of severe behavior problems. *Journal of Applied Behavior Analysis, 23,* 417–429.

Behavior Matrix Worksheet

Settings →	Classroom	Hall	Playground	Cafeteria	Dismissal/Arrival	Bathroom

Expectations

From *Functional Behavioral Assessment and Intervention in Schools: A Practitioner's Guide* (*Grades 1–8*), by J. L. McDougal, S. M. Chafouleas, and B. Waterman, 2006, Champaign, IL: Research Press (800-519-2707; www.researchpress.com)

Survivor Skills Worksheet

Teacher _____ Date _____

Step 1: Teaching

Expectation: _____

_____

Necessary skills: _____

_____

Relevant settings: _____

_____

Step 2: Modeling

List examples: _____

_____

List nonexamples: _____

_____

Describe role-plays: _____

_____

Step 3: Practicing and reinforcing

How and where will practice occur?

_____

_____

How and where will reinforcement occur?

_____

_____

Step 4: Modifying the setting

List setting modifications: _____

_____

Step 5: Generalizing for success

Across which settings and times?

_____

_____

How will training occur?

_____

_____

From *Functional Behavioral Assessment and Intervention in Schools: A Practitioner's Guide (Grades 1–8)*, by J. L. McDougal, S. M. Chafouleas, and B. Waterman, 2006, Champaign, IL: Research Press (800-519-2707; www.researchpress.com)

WORKSHEET 8.3

Targeted Skills Worksheet

Student(s) _____ Date _____

Teacher _____

Type of skill to be taught:

Survival (e.g., listening, following directions, ignoring distractions) ❏

Interpersonal (e.g., sharing, asking permission, learning how to interrupt) ❏

Problem solving (e.g., asking for help, apologizing, setting a goal) ❏

Anger management (e.g., identifying triggers and reducers) ❏

Conflict resolution (e.g., recognizing conflict, negotiation, mediation) ❏

Step 1: Select the behavior and develop a teaching plan.

_____

_____

_____

Considerations:

Have the student(s) ever demonstrated the desired skill? If so, in what situations?

Does cuing help? If so, consider teaching self-monitoring techniques.

How do socially competent peers gain the positive consequence or outcome?

What strengths does the student(s) bring to the learning process?

Step 2: Select students who will participate in the group.

_____

_____

Considerations:

Include both high-status and low-status peers.

Begin with team-building exercises (e.g., naming the group and drawing a picture that illustrates it).

Include some children who are competent in the skill and others who are not.

Step 3: What is the rationale for teaching and using the skill?

_____

_____

Considerations:

Explain the positive outcomes that will be gained and the negatives avoided.

Ensure that the students know the skill and can give a rationale for applying it.

From *Functional Behavioral Assessment and Intervention in Schools: A Practitioner's Guide (Grades 1–8)*, by J. L. McDougal, S. M. Chafouleas, and B. Waterman, 2006, Champaign, IL: Research Press (800-519-2707; www.researchpress.com)

(page 1 of 2)

Step 4: Indicate plan to model the desired behavior (by teacher and competent peers).

_____

_____

_____

Step 5: How will guided practice occur?

_____

_____

Considerations:

Use prompts, guided feedback, and role-play situations.

Fade prompts when students become proficient.

Break skills into smaller components when necessary.

Step 6: Develop a plan for independent practice.

_____

_____

Considerations:

Find ways to reinforce independent skill use.

Identify positive natural consequences for engaging in the skill.

Step 7: Develop a plan to practice in multiple settings.

_____

_____

Considerations:

Where can the student(s) perform the skill in new but similar settings?

How can the behavior be reinforced?

Can the student(s) consistently perform the targeted skill across situations and with different individuals?

Provide prompts and guided practice as needed.

_____

_____

_____

Functional Communication Training Worksheet

Student _____ Date _____

Step 1: Teach

Symbol/cue/phrase: _____

Student need/desire: _____

Step 2: Model

Who will model expected communication? _____

How will the student be prompted? _____

Describe the modeling plan. _____

Step 3: Practice and reinforce

How and where will practice occur? _____

_____

_____

How and where will reinforcement occur? _____

_____

_____

How will negative (target) behavior be addressed? _____

_____

_____

Step 4: Structure the setting

Where will formal training occur (location, duration, time of day)? _____

_____

_____

Step 5: Generalize for success

Across which settings and times? _____

_____

_____

How will training occur? _____

_____

_____

From *Functional Behavioral Assessment and Intervention in Schools: A Practitioner's Guide (Grades 1–8),* by J. L. McDougal, S. M. Chafouleas, and B. Waterman, 2006, Champaign, IL: Research Press (800-519-2707; www.researchpress.com)

CHAPTER 9

Group Interventions

When problem behavior is not limited to one referred student in a given classroom, or when a student is referred for a behavior of low or moderate intensity, a group intervention may be more economical to implement than an individual intervention—in time, effort, and positive benefits. These kinds of interventions represent reasonable strategies for teaching expected alternative behaviors and also for reinforcing and monitoring these prosocial behaviors. Group interventions also are a reasonable way to alter maintaining consequences by creating peer attention or incentive opportunities to support desired behavior.

The following reproducible worksheets appear at the end of this chapter:

> Worksheet 9.1: Lottery Tickets
>
> Worksheet 9.2: Mystery Motivator Chart
>
> Worksheet 9.3: Passport to Success
>
> Worksheet 9.4: Daily Points Recording Form

Why Group Interventions Are Needed

The techniques reviewed in this chapter are designed to motivate and increase positive behavior among groups of students or a whole class. These ideas have been referenced in the literature, and evidence exists to suggest that they are effective. In addition, each has been implemented by the authors and found to be effective in promoting positive student behavior. Most of these interventions are not put into effect over the entire school day or for the entire school year; rather, they are designed to increase positive behavior during particularly important or difficult instructional periods (e.g., language arts) or times of the year (e.g., final exam review, preparing for a standardized test).

Because many of these interventions incentive-based, the first procedure described is one for surveying students' preferences with respect to incentives. After this discussion, the chapter outlines the following group strategies:

> Systematic Praise
>
> Good Behavior Game
>
> Classroom Lottery
>
> Mystery Motivator

Public Posting

Passport to Success

Daily Points System

Brief descriptions of each strategy are included, along with guidelines for use and reproducible forms, when necessary, to facilitate implementation. In addition, a brief key appears with each strategy to provide handy information on appropriate ages, estimated time for implementation, and required materials.

Surveying for Incentive Preferences

Grades: K–8

Time: 10 to 15 minutes

Materials: Chalkboard or easel pad

Because many of the interventions detailed in this section make use of incentives to promote positive behavior, teachers are advised to conduct a preference survey to find out what students would most desire. The following procedure is one way to survey students about their preferred incentives.

Procedure

1. *Have a brainstorming meeting with the class.* During a class meeting, students and teacher brainstorm potential incentive options. Then the teacher writes potential incentives on the chalkboard or easel pad. Some examples:

   Free time at the end of the day

   No-homework passes

   Extra computer time

2. *Fine-tune the list.* Cull from the list ideas that do not appear feasible and develop a list of 10 to 15 feasible incentives.

3. *Survey the class.* After developing the list, have each student list his or her top three preferred incentives in rank order, with number one being most preferred. Score the number of top three votes each incentive received, in addition to the number of times each incentive was ranked in top place.

4. *Compile and report the results.* The most appealing class incentives are those that receive the highest number of top-three and top-place ratings. Report the results to the students and keep a list of the most preferred motivators to reinforce positive classroom behavior.

> ### IMPLEMENTATION TIPS
>
> To make incentive-based plans more effective, consider the following:
>
> - *Student choice.* Consider allowing students to choose among two or three options.
>
> - *Reassessments.* Periodically survey the class or introduce new ideas so that incentives do not lose appeal.
>
> - *Individualized plans.* Students who do not respond to group contingencies or incentives may require individual assessment.

Group Interventions

Systematic Praise

Grades: K–8

Time: Periodic 15- to 20-minute observations throughout the day

Materials: Paper and pencil (for the observer)

This intervention is appealing to many educators because it is relatively easy to implement and involves no extra resources and little in the way of additional time. The basic idea is that if teacher attention reinforces behavior, then teacher attention to positive behavior should increase desired responses. The intervention involves the participation of someone who will observe the interaction between teacher and students (e.g., school social worker or psychologist, or another teacher who has received training in observation).

Procedure

1. *Define the behaviors of concern.* Prioritize, reduce to an observable number, and define each. For example, the following behaviors may be chosen and defined:

   Calling out during instruction. Talking out without raising your hand and being called on.

   Disrupting instruction. Making noises or behaving in a way that interrupts the teacher and interferes with the learning of other students—for example, banging desks, poking peers, making unnecessary noises, and throwing objects.

2. *Observe the classroom.* Conduct two or three classroom observations (of 15 to 20 minutes each) during periods of direct instruction. On a sheet of paper, record the behaviors of concern (e.g., number of call-outs per hour) as well as each teacher verbalization as positive ("I like the way you . . ." "I'd like to thank the class for . . ."); neutral/instructional ("Please take out your books and turn to page 104" "Raymond, I have your lunch money at my desk");

or negative (redirections, warnings, and indications of discontent—"Julie, I asked you not to do that"). Then record both the number of target behaviors and calculate the ratio of positive to negative teacher comments.

3. *Report back to the teacher.* Try a format like "You were right! My observations indicate that you deal with an average of [insert the number of call-outs you observed] call-outs per hour. The other thing I observed is that all of this misbehavior draws a good deal of your attention. In fact, my observations indicate that you attend to negative behaviors, on average, [insert your ratio here] as often as you comment on positive behavior."

4. *Seek commitment to intervene and evaluate effectiveness.* For the next few days, ask the teacher to think about his or her comments to the class as positive or negative. For the trial period, ask the teacher to consciously give the class at least two praise statements for each negative redirection or comment made. Repeat Steps 2 and 3 to assess how well simply increasing attention to positive behavior can improve student behavior and decrease class disruption.

Good Behavior Game

Grades: K–5

Time: 1–2 hours per day

Materials: Chalkboard or easel pad, agreed-upon incentives

The Good Behavior Game is a simple technique to create peer pressure to promote positive behaviors in the classroom. It is a type of *group contingency*—in this case, a reward given based on group performance. This strategy involves splitting the class into two or more teams, defining behaviors that will be rewarded, recording the performance of each group, and providing incentives to those team members who have met the criteria.

Procedure

1. *Define and publicly post the behaviors you wish to decrease.* For example:

   Calling out during instruction. Talking out without raising your hand or being called on

   Disrupting instruction. Making noises or behaving in a way that interrupts the teacher and interferes with the learning of other students

   Being noncompliant. Not following teacher directions in a reasonable amount of time

2. *Divide the class into teams.* You may divide the class into teams based on these characteristics:

   Seating arrangement. Create two teams of students, sitting in the left half and the right half of the room, or four teams, one for each cluster of desks.

   Class composition. Consider equalizing teams in number of challenging and compliant children.

3. *Identify incentives to be awarded to teams that meet expectations.* Brainstorm a list of potential incentives and a time when they can be given. (For more details, see the previous section of this chapter on surveying for incentive preferences.)

4. *Create a system for recording points and set the performance criterion.* Develop an easy method for recording information for each team. General scoring rules are as follows: Points are tallied by the teacher as they occur (e.g., if a student on Team A calls out without raising her hand, the teacher administers a point to team A). Points are generally administered without discussion; any unwarranted debate may result in another point being given. Any infraction of the desired behaviors by any individual on the team gets one point. If desired, special bonus points—that is, subtracting one of the given points—may be awarded to a team displaying exemplary behavior.

5. *Determine the criterion for receiving the incentive.* One common method is to award the incentive only to the team with the least number of total points. Or all teams with point totals below a predetermined level may be given the incentive.

It should be noted that variations are possible in the delivery of incentives. In fact, the type of contingency may be randomized on a daily basis (Theodore, Bray, Kehle, & Jenson, 2000). In this case, the teacher randomly selects the type of contingency the class is working for each day. There are three options for group contingencies:

Dependent. The incentive is provided to all team members if a randomly selected team member meets the criterion.

Interdependent. The incentive is provided to all team members if all students on the team meet the criterion.

Independent. The incentive is provided on an individual basis if the student meets the criterion.

6. *Decide when to play the game.* Generally, the Good Behavior Game should be reserved for those academic times that are instructionally most important to teachers or those that are most problematic. This technique should not be overused because it can lose its appeal. As a general rule of thumb, teachers should play the game during times of direct instruction and not for more than about an hour each day.

7. *Prepare the class.* Review the selected behaviors, agree on the rewards, specify the time the game will be played, and select teams. Then write the team names on the chalkboard or easel pad. (Students may want to select team names; if not, just use Team A, Team B, etc.)

8. *Play.* With everything in place, inform the students when you are starting the game (and when you are concluding it). All displays of the specified behaviors result in a point for the team. Do not spend long periods of time attending to negative behavior; simply specify the infraction (one point for calling out), score the penalty point, and resume instruction. Any arguing or disruptive displays of disapproval result in another point.

IMPLEMENTATION TIPS

Here are some easy solutions for the most common problems that occur in the Good Behavior Game:

- *The "I'm-gonna-ruin-it-for-others" syndrome.* If one student or a small group of students are finding it amusing to generate numerous points for their team, simply form another team with those students (or even just one student) and have them take the points they accumulated to the new team. These students should be allowed to earn their way back onto the original team but should not be allowed to spoil the game for others.

- *"I don't want that dumb old sticker anyway!"* If the game seems to be losing its appeal, consider (a) changing incentives or making the reinforcer unknown prior to the game (draw from a jar), (b) allowing winning students to choose among a list of possible rewards, (c) adding weekly rewards for teams meeting the daily criterion, or (d) randomizing the type of contingency used (see Step 5).

- *The special case.* Some students will consistently not respond to the Good Behavior Game. This may be due to difficulties with emotional/behavioral regulation, academic frustration, or other personal issues. For these students, an individualized intervention plan may be warranted in order to provide extra support to participate in the game. Some may even need to be accommodated with alternative intervention methods.

Classroom Lottery

Grades: K–8

Time: A few minutes per day

Materials: Lottery Tickets, jar or other container, poster board and markers (to make an "Expectations Board"), agreed-upon incentives

In this intervention, lottery tickets are paired with praise to reinforce positive behavior in the classroom. Tickets are given to students who exhibit specified behaviors, such as being on-task, completing homework, helping others, or being kind. Students write their names on earned lottery tickets and put them in a container in the classroom. The teacher holds drawings at preset or random intervals (hourly, daily, weekly) for prizes or privileges (e.g., serving as line leader, taking attendance to the office). A big drawing at the end of the day might even decide the lucky student who gets to cut out the lottery tickets for the following day! A reproducible page of tickets appears as Worksheet 9.1, at the end of this chapter.

Procedure

1. *Define and post behaviors you wish to increase.* Write these behaviors on an "Expectations Board," provide examples to students, and display the list of behaviors in a highly visible location in the classroom.

2. *Select or design the tickets you will use.* Sometimes having the class select among a few options increases their interest.

3. *Decide when to hold drawings.* You may want to determine specific times during the day or week, have random drawings, or have a combination of these approaches.

4. *When first implementing the program, be generous with tickets and drawings.* Decrease frequency over time. Remember, the lottery is an incentive only if students earn the tickets! In the beginning, reinforce positive behaviors frequently and hold drawings at least daily (or several times a day, if feasible).

IMPLEMENTATION TIPS

To make the classroom lottery most effective, consider the following ideas:

- When awarding tickets, be sure to specify the behavior being rewarded and praise the student for the behavior.

- Reinforce both generally well-behaved students and those who are most improved.

- Evaluate the effectiveness of the program every few weeks. If student behavior is excellent, consider reducing the frequency of tickets and drawings. If more positive behavior is desired, increase the frequency of tickets and drawings.

- Come up with new reinforcements frequently. Consider the use of special roles, responsibilities, and privileges (e.g., line leader, attendance runner, student to help kindergartners prepare for dismissal). These reinforcers usually have more sustained appeal than tangible ones.

Mystery Motivator

Grades: K–8

Time: 15 to 20 minutes per day or week

Materials: Paper, special markers with an invisible ink color that appears when another marker writes over it; a large envelope (for the "Incentives Envelope"); poster board and markers (to make an "Expectations Board"); the Mystery Motivator Chart; agreed-upon incentives

The Mystery Motivator is a classwide approach for delivering random reinforcement for appropriate student behaviors. The appeal of this intervention is twofold: (a) the whole class must perform in order to receive an end-of-the-day incentive and (b) the class never knows when they might receive the incentive. A Mystery Motivator Chart appears as Worksheet 9.2, at the end of the chapter.

Procedure

1. *Design and post the behaviors you wish to increase on the Expectations Board.* Consider what you want the class to do in order to earn the Mystery Motivator (e.g., be on time and prepared for class, follow class rules). Write these behaviors on the board, provide examples to students, and display the board in a visible location in the classroom.

2. *With the entire class, brainstorm a list of potential incentives that may be earned at the end of the day.* Make sure that the incentives are viewed as rewards by all students and are feasible for use in the classroom (i.e., they don't require a lot of money or time). Write each incentive on a separate sheet of paper and fold the paper to produce the secret (mystery) incentive option. Place the incentive options in a hat or other container.

3. *Create an Incentives Envelope.* Select a large envelope; consider decorating it yourself or having students in the class decorate it. The envelope will be used to hold the secret incentive that is randomly drawn by a student. This envelope can be displayed at the front of the classroom (some teachers hang it from a line off the ceiling outside the normal reach of students).

4. *Prominently display a Mystery Motivator Chart at the front of the class.* The Mystery Motivator Chart is displayed in the front of the class, generally out of students' reach. At the beginning of each week, select the days of the week that will be Mystery Motivator days and, with the invisible ink markers, write an *M* in the square under those days. (The days not to be rewarded are left blank.)

   Initially, three or four days per week may be reward days. Gradually, the number of reward days can be reduced to one or two days. When selecting days, also consider consecutive reward days during some weeks to prohibit students from "slacking off" the day after they have received a motivator.

5. *Play the game.* With all of the materials for the Mystery Motivator game displayed at the front of the classroom, use the game as a cue to help settle the class when they become unruly (e.g., "Class, this is quiet reading time, and I don't want to hear any talking. Remember, we need to follow the rules to get our Mystery Motivator").

   At the end of the day, select a student to color in the space on the Mystery Motivator Worksheet corresponding to the day of the week. (Make sure that students know that cheating by coloring out of the lines to explore the next day could result in the loss of reward!) If it is not a reward day, congratulate the class on their good behavior and perhaps allow them some free time to chat. Also remind them that it may be more likely that the reward day is tomorrow so they should be extra careful. If a reward day is uncovered, select another student to open the Incentives Envelope and read aloud what the class has won. Congratulate the students and enjoy the incentive time.

If the class is not well behaved and does not earn the Mystery Motivator, they do not participate in the festivities, and quiet time to complete work may be provided (which also should leave them wondering whether they would have received a reward that day).

Note that bonus points and secret messages are good ways to add some appeal to this game. In the "Bonus Box" on the worksheet, the teacher can write, with invisible ink, additional incentives to be earned at the end of the week or can write a number of additional minutes of incentive time to be added for good behavior all week. In the "Secret Message" section, teachers can use invisible ink to write an extra incentive choice, give a homework pass, and so on. Students may only expose the secret message if they earned the motivator all week.

IMPLEMENTATION TIPS

To make the Mystery Motivator most effective, consider the following ideas:

- For those students not trying as hard as they might, consider making a separate team or using individual Mystery Motivator Worksheets. This will allow other students to ignore the inappropriate behavior of one or a few students.

- If students complain about the incentive earned, create a rule that any complaints or requests for different rewards will result in a loss of the reward for that day.

- If students become unruly because they had good behavior but did not earn a reward that day, you may always reserve the right to suspend the game for the next day or the rest of the week.

Public Posting

Grades: K–8

Time: 5 to 10 minutes per day

Materials: Poster board and markers, tracking emblem, incentives (if desired)

Public posting involves the public display of (and thus increased attention to) student performance on some prespecified academic or behavioral measure of progress. For example, public posting can be used to increase desired behaviors like homework and assignment completion, being on time and prepared for class, and time-on-task rates. In fact, because of its effectiveness, public posting is also used to increase desired behaviors in industry, such as postings of the number of days without a safety violation or the number of units per hour assembled by a group of workers.

Procedure

1. *Decide on the behavior or academic response to be monitored.* Select and define the academic or behavioral responses to be monitored and publicly displayed.

2. *Develop a board to post student performance.* Develop a board to be displayed in the classroom to allow students to visually track their performance. The board should include (a) the behavior being monitored; (b) each student's name, written down the vertical axis, and (c) spaces corresponding to the days of the week across the horizontal axis. When designing the boards, the bigger and flashier the better. Also consider having students help construct and decorate the board.

3. *Decide on a tracking emblem and procedure.* Decide how and when progress will be indicated on the board. Suggestions include stars, stamps, stickers, or personalized icons that students can affix to the board. Behavior may be recorded after completion of an assignment or display of the desired behavior. Select at least one specific daily measure and ensure immediate feedback to students to promote positive behavior.

IMPLEMENTATION TIPS

To make public posting most effective, consider these suggestions:

- Compare students' performance to their own past performance (not to the performance of others).

- Add a reward for specific levels of performance or personal improvement.

- Consider a team-based approach: Split the class into teams and have a public competition.

- Incorporate a class-selected theme for the posting board (e.g., the World Series of exam review).

- Use large boards, color, decorations, and student art and ideas in the activity.

- Display the posting to visitors: Invite outside members of the school and community to come in and view the board.

- Consider adding a school-home component, whereby students meeting predetermined levels of performance receive a positive note home.

Passport to Success

Grades: 4–8

Time: 45 to 60 minutes per week

Materials: Passport to Success, individual ink stamps for each participating teacher

The Passport to Success is one option for teams of teachers to organize an approach to classwide discipline. The strategy works best if teams meet on a regular basis to review student progress and incentive options, and discuss strategies for students who are not responding to the intervention. Figure 9.1 shows a passport including common classroom goals. A blank version appears as Worksheet 9.3.

In the intervention, students carry their passports in assignment notebooks that transition with them to each class. Each teacher on the team has a personalized ink stamp that is used to stamp each behavioral infraction in the corresponding area of the passport. Students receiving, for example, seven or more stamps during a given passport interval are not able to participate in the incentive time with the others. Instead, they may be assigned to a quiet study hall to complete schoolwork.

Procedure

1. *As a team, identify behavioral expectations.* Also select the behaviors for which an infraction stamp will be issued. These will be listed on the student passport, as in the sample shown in Figure 9.1. (A blank version of the passport appears as Worksheet 9.3, at the end of this chapter.)

2. *Design the passport.* Generally, the passport defines behavioral goals and expectations along the left margin and includes an area for infraction stamps on the right.

3. *Determine the incentives.* Incentives are selected from a student preference survey among those deemed reasonable by the school faculty. Activities available during the incentive period are announced during the first class period beginning each passport period (e.g., Monday morning).

4. *Determine the duration of each passport interval.* For example, teachers may want to start with weekly incentives and slowly fade them to one or two times per month.

5. *Review the following guidelines with students:*

    You are responsible for carrying your passport with you at all times.

    If you are absent from school, you are responsible for all assigned work. Any work not completed will be turned into stamps on your passport.

    Whenever one of the specified behaviors is not followed, you will receive a stamp in your passport from a team teacher. Certain infractions are an automatic seven stamps. These are skipping class, truancy, fighting, and other serious disciplinary infractions resulting in suspension.

FIGURE 9.1

Sample Passport to Success

Student ___*Benjamin*___   Collection date ___*3/16/06*___

GOALS	STAMPS*
Homework • on time • complete	
Prepared • all materials • books, pens, pencils • papers, worksheets	
On Time • in seat before bell rings	
Successful Behavior • working, on-task • appropriate language • respecting self, others, and property	

* 7 Stamps = No participation in reward

Passports will be collected during the first class period at the end of the passport interval (e.g., Friday morning).

If you receive fewer than seven points you will be allowed access to the incentive. Students with seven or more points will be assigned to study hall to complete classwork.

6. *Implement the program.*

IMPLEMENTATION TIPS

To make the passport intervention most effective, consider the following:

- *Team meeting.* The first step is for teachers to meet as a team to decide on the behaviors that need to be emphasized, the length of the interval to be reinforced (not more than two weeks is recommended), and the procedures or persons responsible for reviewing student progress.

- *Incentives.* The last period of the day at the end of the passport period is generally incentive time. Passports are collected during the first period of the incentive day, and students are assigned to either incentive time or study hall. Some teams use student survey information to help them select the incentive activities. (See the suggestions for conducting student surveys earlier in this chapter.) Generally, movies with popcorn, computer games, pizza parties, free time, extra gym time, and outside recess are high on the list of student incentives. Teacher teams may wish to offer different incentive activities in each of their classrooms to provide students with a choice.

- *Consequences.* Make sure that students who have not earned the incentive time have a quiet study hall or other neutral place to go while the rest of the students "whoop it up!"

- *Modifications.* You may want to increase the appeal of incentives (by asking students what they would like) or shorten the passport period (use a weekly rather than biweekly incentive or refer to the passport as a warning to redirect students).

- *Individualized plans.* If a student is consistently not responding to the passport approach, consider developing and using an individualized plan.

Daily Points System

Grades: K–8

Time: 20 minutes per day

Materials: Poster board and markers (for the "Expectations Board"), Daily Points Recording Form, agreed-upon incentives

Points systems can effectively increase desired behaviors, such as homework completion, academic responding, and appropriate social behaviors. These systems couple praise and awarding of points to reinforce desired behaviors. Public posting of the points also boosts its appeal. A Daily Points Recording Form is given as Worksheet 9.4.

Procedure

1. *Define and post behaviors you wish to increase on the "Expectations Board."* Identify the positive behaviors to be targeted and how many points will be earned. For example, students might earn up to three points per academic period or half day (one point each) for following directions, respecting others, and completing assigned work. In addition, students might earn bonus points for sharing, cooperating, and walking away from conflict. Write the desired behaviors on the poster board, provide students with examples, and display the board in a visible location in the classroom.

2. *Develop a procedure for administering points.* Some teachers have issued points in a class meeting format, where all students are asked which score they believe they earned and the teacher plays the part of scorekeeper and referee. Other procedures may include simply having the teacher or other adult in the classroom do the scoring after predetermined intervals.

3. *Identify incentives.* Generate a list of incentive options and the cost of each with the class. Try to identify both short-term (daily) options and larger (weekly) ones.

4. *Keep track of student performance on the Daily Points Recording Form.*

5. *Decide on a time to compute points and administer incentives.* If desired, select specific times of the day or week to compute points and incentives (e.g., at the end of the day, prior to dismissal). Consider allowing students to compute their own points and choose incentives based on their earnings.

6. *When first implementing the program, be liberal in awarding points.* Remember, incentives are only appealing if students earn them. In the beginning, try to reinforce positive behaviors frequently and praise those students doing well with the system.

IMPLEMENTATION TIPS

To make the daily points system most effective, consider the following suggestions:

- When awarding points, be sure to specify the behavior being rewarded and praise the student.

- Evaluate your program every few weeks. If more positive behavior is desired, try (a) altering incentive options, (b) increasing use of bonus points, or (c) having a "special auction" or other buying event. Special auction times can be implemented when students have a unique opportunity (e.g., when you are looking for a line leader or attendance runner, or the librarian needs a hand). An auction is a fun and interesting way for students to use their points. These auctions can have more than one winner, or the lucky student might be allowed to bring a buddy.

- Add a cost component. To decrease the occurrence of specific negative behaviors, consider adding a limited cost component. That is, for specific behaviors such as swearing or disrupting the class, students may lose a predetermined number of points for that day or period. However, caution is warranted when using this approach; students should not lose everything during one rapid downhill behavioral slide. This will almost guarantee loss of interest in the system.

Lottery Tickets

GREAT JOB TICKET ★ AWARDED TO: _____	GREAT JOB TICKET ★ AWARDED TO: _____	GREAT JOB TICKET ★ AWARDED TO: _____
GREAT JOB TICKET ★ AWARDED TO: _____	GREAT JOB TICKET ★ AWARDED TO: _____	GREAT JOB TICKET ★ AWARDED TO: _____
GREAT JOB TICKET ★ AWARDED TO: _____	GREAT JOB TICKET ★ AWARDED TO: _____	GREAT JOB TICKET ★ AWARDED TO: _____
GREAT JOB TICKET ★ AWARDED TO: _____	GREAT JOB TICKET ★ AWARDED TO: _____	GREAT JOB TICKET ★ AWARDED TO: _____

From *Functional Behavioral Assessment and Intervention in Schools: A Practitioner's Guide (Grades 1–8),* by J. L. McDougal, S. M. Chafouleas, and B. Waterman, 2006, Champaign, IL: Research Press (800-519-2707; www.researchpress.com)

Mystery Motivator Chart

MY MYSTERY MOTIVATOR IS SO BRIGHT, I'M GONNA NEED MY SHADES!!

MON	TUE	WED	THUR	FRI	BONUS

SECRET MESSAGES:

From *Functional Behavioral Assessment and Intervention in Schools: A Practitioner's Guide (Grades 1–8),* by J. L. McDougal, S. M. Chafouleas, and B. Waterman, 2006, Champaign, IL: Research Press (800-519-2707; www.researchpress.com)

Passport to Success

Student _____   Collection date _____

GOALS	STAMPS

From *Functional Behavioral Assessment and Intervention in Schools: A Practitioner's Guide (Grades 1–8)*, by J. L. McDougal, S. M. Chafouleas, and B. Waterman, 2006, Champaign, IL: Research Press (800-519-2707; www.researchpress.com)

Daily Points Recording Form

Circle Points Earned per Class

STUDENTS							BONUS	TOTAL
	1 2 3	1 2 3	1 2 3	1 2 3	1 2 3	1 2 3		
	1 2 3	1 2 3	1 2 3	1 2 3	1 2 3	1 2 3		
	1 2 3	1 2 3	1 2 3	1 2 3	1 2 3	1 2 3		
	1 2 3	1 2 3	1 2 3	1 2 3	1 2 3	1 2 3		
	1 2 3	1 2 3	1 2 3	1 2 3	1 2 3	1 2 3		
	1 2 3	1 2 3	1 2 3	1 2 3	1 2 3	1 2 3		
	1 2 3	1 2 3	1 2 3	1 2 3	1 2 3	1 2 3		
	1 2 3	1 2 3	1 2 3	1 2 3	1 2 3	1 2 3		
	1 2 3	1 2 3	1 2 3	1 2 3	1 2 3	1 2 3		
	1 2 3	1 2 3	1 2 3	1 2 3	1 2 3	1 2 3		
	1 2 3	1 2 3	1 2 3	1 2 3	1 2 3	1 2 3		
	1 2 3	1 2 3	1 2 3	1 2 3	1 2 3	1 2 3		
	1 2 3	1 2 3	1 2 3	1 2 3	1 2 3	1 2 3		
	1 2 3	1 2 3	1 2 3	1 2 3	1 2 3	1 2 3		

CHAPTER 10

Individual Interventions

This chapter focuses on intervention techniques to promote positive behavior among individual students. All of the techniques outlined here have been supported by research and documented in the literature. Each has also been implemented by the authors and found to be effective in promoting positive student behavior (e.g., McDougal, Clonan, & Martens, 2002; McDougal, Nastasi, & Chafouleas, 2005).

It is assumed that the use of a particular intervention described in this chapter is (a) based on an assessment of the environmental conditions supporting or predicting the student's behavior, (b) perceived by the teacher as feasible for use in the classroom, and (c) implemented for high-intensity behaviors or those behaviors persisting despite well-implemented classwide interventions. In addition, it is expected that the interventions will not be permanent. In other words, although the initial goal is to demonstrate positive behavioral change, it also is important to continue to monitor progress and fade intervention procedures over time.

The information provided here will guide reliable implementation of each strategy and assist educators in altering the consequences for problem behavior while promoting and reinforcing alternate behaviors. Some guidelines for selecting an intervention based on behavioral function appear in Table 6.3, titled "Intervention Ideas by Behavioral Function." The interventions shown here are not intended as an exhaustive list. Instead, this is a concise guide to some effective strategies for use in the schools. We encourage creative modification of any of these protocols, as long as the procedures are well specified and in keeping with the intervention criteria described in chapter 7. For additional ideas, visit http://www.interventioncentral.com or see *The Tough Kid Tool Box* (Jenson, Rhode, & Reavis, 1994).

The following reproducible worksheets appear at the end of this chapter:

Worksheet 10.1: Self-Monitoring Planning Guide

Worksheet 10.2: Daily Self-Monitoring Form 1

Worksheet 10.3: Daily Self-Monitoring Form 2

Worksheet 10.4: Daily Self-Monitoring Form 3

Worksheet 10.5: Daily Self-Monitoring Form 4

Worksheet 10.6: Weekly Self-Monitoring Form 1

Worksheet 10.7: Weekly Self-Monitoring Form 2

Worksheet 10.8: Behavior Contract Planning Guide

Worksheet 10.9: Behavior Contract 1

Worksheet 10.10: Behavior Contract 2

Why Individual Interventions Are Needed

When considering implementing a behavioral intervention for an individual student, it is important to remember that teaching, modeling, and reinforcement are much more effective than punishment in promoting positive behavior. Furthermore, although incentives are helpful when the intervention is first implemented, they should gradually be replaced by social roles, responsibilities, and privileges. Finally, changing an individual student's behavior is hard work. Well-designed interventions are often effective but not without significant time, energy, and adherence to agreed-upon procedures. Effective interventions for individual students have the following characteristics:

They focus on altering predictive conditions to prevent the occurrence of a child's problem behavior.

They provide direct instruction, modeling, and support to address identified skill deficits and teach alternative replacement behaviors.

They consider the function of the student's behavior to aid in the design of consequent strategies so that the alternate replacement behavior is followed by the maintaining consequence and the problem behavior is no longer reinforced.

They are socially valid and, whenever possible, involve the parent, student, and teacher in the intervention design.

They contain components that are clear, explicit, and consistently applied.

They are formatively assessed and revised, based on intervention effectiveness.

In addition, intervention effectiveness may be increased by doing the following:

Reteaching the child the desired behavior or skill.

Increasing the amount of instructional or social support.

Increasing the frequency or duration of the incentive (e.g., giving the incentive daily rather than weekly).

Using rewards that are more appealing to the student (e.g., based on a preference survey).

Involving the parents and adding a home component.

Reviewing the maintaining consequences to ensure that negative behavior is no longer functional.

Individual Interventions

This section of the chapter describes the following specific individual interventions: self-monitoring, behavior contracts, time-outs, and school-home notes. Each strategy is described briefly, and guidelines for use are given. Reproducible forms are included at the end of the chapter to facilitate implementation of the interventions. In addition, each strategy is accompanied by a brief key that provides information on appropriate ages, estimated time for implementation, and required materials.

Self-Monitoring

Grades: K–8

Time: 5 to 10 minutes per day

Materials: Self-Monitoring Planning Guide (Worksheet 10.1); self-monitoring form of your choice (see Worksheets 10.2–10.7)

In self-monitoring, students periodically rate their own behaviors. Target behaviors may be either desirable or undesirable behaviors. Self-monitoring can be of benefit to both the teacher and the student. This strategy can reduce the time the teacher spends observing and recording student behaviors. Furthermore, self-monitoring procedures are often useful for managing student behaviors outside of the classroom setting because behavioral expectations across a variety of settings can be tied to a single classroom reinforcement program. Finally, students may actually be more reliable monitors of their own behaviors than the teacher because, unlike the teacher, they are always present during their behavioral displays!

For students, self-monitoring also has distinct advantages. The activity of monitoring their own behaviors may help children learn to understand and self-regulate acceptable classroom behavior. When the teacher involves students in the creation of a self-monitoring program, they often have a greater investment in abiding by the rules of the program.

Procedure

1. *Determine method of measurement.* Students may record their behaviors in several ways: placing a check mark on a chart, clicking a wrist-counter, or circling an item on a self-evaluation sheet, for example.

2. *Choose the type of self-monitoring program.* There are two main types of self-monitoring programs. First, teachers may create a self-monitoring program in which the student rates current behavior when a signal is given. For example, the teacher may set a kitchen timer and have the student rate his on-task behavior when it rings. If you use this system, it is important that the signal not distract others and that the intervals between signals vary randomly. The

second, easier procedure is to have students rate themselves at the end of naturally occurring intervals (or academic periods) in the daily schedule.

3. *Check for accuracy.* Any self-monitoring procedure should include occasional teacher checks of student ratings to ensure that the student's ratings are accurate. Student self-monitoring is more accurate when the student has clearly learned which behaviors to monitor.

4. *Consider the need for incentives.* Self-monitoring is effective in many cases without including any additional rewards. However, when it is tied to another behavioral intervention, such as positive reinforcement, the impact can be considerably greater.

IMPLEMENTATION TIPS

To make self-monitoring more effective, consider the following:

- *Additional components.* Self-monitoring is easy to combine with other interventions to create a more effective package. For example, daily self-monitoring forms might be sent home as part of a school-home component, the procedure might be combined with a student contract and incentive program, or the monitoring might be tracked over time and linked with weekly or monthly incentives.

- *Student participation.* It is helpful to involve students in the creation of monitoring plans and forms. They can select or draw icons depicting good and poor behavior for their monitoring sheets, design feasible and preferred incentive options, and share positive daily ratings with teachers and other staff members in the building.

- *Bonus ideas.* A bonus clause may be created for especially good ratings (e.g., great all day or all week). So, if students get at least three out of four great ratings per day, they get free time. If they get four or more great ratings a day, the bonus might be to allow them to bring a friend to share the free time.

Behavior Contracts

Grades: K–8

Time: 20 minutes setup, 5 minutes per day

Materials: Behavior Contract Planning Guide (Worksheet 10.8), behavior contract of your choice (see Worksheets 10.9–10.10), agreed-upon incentives

A behavior contract, also called a contingency contract, is an agreement between a student and teacher (or parent, administrator, or any other interested party) that designates (a) the behaviors expected of the student and (b) the incentives that will be provided to the student if those behaviors are exhibited. Generally, behavior contracts are comprehensive agreements in that specific incentives for positive behaviors as well as consequences for negative behaviors are indicated. As a result, behavior contracts can be combined with other intervention ideas, such as self-monitoring or time-out. Behavior contracts are most useful for producing small, successive increments of positive change when used with students who are capable of monitoring their own behavior.

Procedure

1. *Decide which behaviors the student will be expected to perform.* The behaviors should be defined in clear, observable terms and stated positively, in goal form. For example, "Billy will complete 80 percent of assigned class work each day."

2. *Identify the incentives that will be delivered to the student for performing the appropriate behaviors.* The rewards should be selected by both the student and teacher, and should be both appealing to the student and feasible for the teacher.

3. *Determine when and how rewards will be delivered to the student.*

4. *Consider adding consequences for failure to meet the minimum level of performance.* Although these consequences are optional, they may boost the effectiveness of the procedure.

5. *Consider including a bonus clause in the contract.* This clause provides a "bonus incentive" for outstanding performance. Although this incentive is optional, it too may boost the effectiveness of the procedure.

6. *Decide when the contract will begin and end.*

7. *Complete the agreement through a process of discussion and signing of the contract.* This discussion process includes eliciting the student's input during the contract development and clearly identifying the teacher's expectations.

IMPLEMENTATION TIPS

To make behavior contracts more effective, consider the following:

- *Parent involvement.* Facilitate parent involvement and consider using a daily school-home note to keep parents informed.

- *Periodic evaluation.* Make sure to set a review date with the student to evaluate the effectiveness of the contract. Typically, the agreement can be reviewed within two weeks, and minor revisions can be made then to increase feasibility and effectiveness.

Time-Out

Grades: K–8

Time: 5 to 30 minutes

Materials: Time-Out Planning Guide (Worksheet 10.11), Time-Out Supervisor's Guide (Worksheet 10.12)

Time-out is a frequently used (and sometimes abused) intervention procedure implemented as a consequence for disruptive, noncompliant, and unsafe behavior. It is a useful technique for decreasing negative attention-seeking behaviors and behaviors such as tantrums. Time-out should be reserved for challenging behaviors that cannot be tolerated in the classroom. Other, less intense behaviors may be addressed with a more positive intervention. In addition, although the specific focus of time-out is reducing certain behaviors, it should be considered in conjunction with incentive procedures aimed at increasing appropriate replacement behaviors.

Procedure

1. *Consider time-in.* Before developing a time-out intervention, it is important to consider the "time-in" environment. Adequate opportunity for positive interaction and reinforcement in the classroom is critical. In essence, time-out can only be expected to be an effective intervention component if classroom time is desirable to the student. Chapter 9 lists several classwide interventions that help improve the appeal of time-in.

2. *Consider the function.* When deciding whether to use time-out, educators should first consider the function of the behavior problem. For instance, time-out is not likely to be effective with students who misbehave in order to get out of doing their schoolwork or with students who act out so they can leave the classroom (escape-related behaviors). In addition, time-out would be a poor consequence for self-reinforcing behaviors, such as rocking and flapping, because it would allow the student greater opportunity to express these behaviors.

3. *Explain why, where, and when.* Before implementing the time-out, the student must be instructed in the problem behaviors that will result in time-out and the procedures that will be followed. Once the procedures have been explained, the protocol should be implemented in a calm, matter-of-fact manner, with limited teacher attention and without extraneous discussion. Before students go to time-out, they should be told what behavior they exhibited, what they must do while in time-out (e.g., sit quietly, don't talk, do an assignment), and how long time-out will last (a rule of thumb is one minute for each year of age, either chronological or emotional). Time-out should not last very long, particularly if time-in is rewarding. Finally, time-out should occur immediately after the exhibited negative behavior. Having a student "do time" for an offense that occurred the day before is less likely to be effective than an immediate consequence.

4. *Ensure proper reentry.* At the end of the time-out period, students may reenter the classroom if they have demonstrated appropriate behavior, such as appearing calm and coming in appropriately (e.g., walking back quietly, not entering kicking or swearing). If not, students should not be allowed to reenter the class. If students have difficulty successfully transitioning from time-out to class, they can complete some academic work in the time-out area to get behavioral momentum going in the right direction prior to reentry.

5. *Consider parent contact.* If a students' behavior is disruptive enough to warrant time-out, parent contact is advised. Parents should be made aware of the time-out procedure and contacted each time it is implemented with their child.

IMPLEMENTATION TIPS

To make time-outs more effective, consider the following circumstances:

- *The student talks-out or is otherwise disruptive.* If the student sits quietly in time-out for a few minutes and then becomes disruptive or speaks out, reset the timer and begin the time-out period again.

- *The student refuses to go to time-out.* Let the student know that for each minute he refuses to go, time will be added to the time-out period. Cue the student every minute or so ("[Student], now you're up to six minutes; you need to go to the time-out area"). If the student continues to refuse after several minutes, then another consequence should be used (e.g., call home, loss of free time, detention, office referral).

- *The student becomes aggressive when required to go to time-out.* Aggressive students require additional resources, a crisis plan, and careful consideration of both district policy and educational regulations. Time-out options range from removing the rest of the class so that the student stays in the classroom to having building staff trained and certified in a form of nonviolent physical crisis intervention safely escort and contain the student in a time-out room until calm. *Considerable caution here is advised.*

School-Home Notes

Grades: K–8

Time: 5 minutes per day

Materials: School-Home Note Planning Guide (Worksheet 10.13), School-Home Note (Worksheet 10.14), School-Home Progress Monitoring Graph (Worksheet 10.15)

School-home notes, a version of daily behavior report cards, have been used in the classroom both as an intervention and as a monitoring device (Chafouleas, Riley-Tillman, & McDougal, 2002). Usually, these notes include one or more specified behaviors that are rated by the teacher at least daily.

The note provides frequent feedback on the child's behavior at school. Often these notes are used in the context of a home-based reinforcement system, in which the child may earn an incentive (e.g., extra TV time) for good school behavior. The authors have also used the notes to provide a student with a home-based consequence for negative school behavior (poor ratings, failure to bring note home), such as removing the child's access to preferred activities (e.g., video games, roller blades).

In addition to being an effective behavioral intervention, daily notes may be used to monitor student behavior over time. For example, ratings prior to the intervention can be collected to help determine appropriate goals, and the goals can then be written to correspond with the type of daily rating used—for example, "by the end of March, Johanna will consistently earn teacher ratings of 4 out of 5 for compliance and positive peer interaction."

Procedure

1. *Design the school-home note.* Decide which behaviors the student will be expected to perform. The behaviors should be defined in clear, observable terms and discussed with the student. The School-Home Note Planning Guide, shown in Worksheet 10.13, specifies considerations in this process.

2. *Observe and rate the student's behavior.* Every day, the teacher rates each specific behavior and briefly discusses results with the student. At the end of the day, the student is given a copy of the note to take home. (It is a good idea for the teacher to keep a copy on file.) After parents review the note, they sign it, and the student returns it to the teacher the next morning. This process maintains daily communication between home and school. Worksheet 10.14 involves three common school issues: work completion, peer interaction, and compliance.

3. *Monitor progress over time.* An easy-to-use monitoring form, shown in Worksheet 10.15, can be used to graph the ratings on school-home notes over time and thus assess progress. To complete the graph, simply list the behavior to be monitored in the "behavior box" and record each daily rating over time. To provide additional motivation, consider allowing the student to participate in graphing daily progress or offer additional rewards for meeting weekly performance goals.

> **IMPLEMENTATION TIPS**
>
> To make school-home notes more effective, consider the following:
>
> - *Combine with other intervention components.* A student contract, home and school incentives, and a weekly or monthly bonus for sustained progress may be used along with the school-home note.
>
> - *Set goals.* If an incentive program is added, you may want to rate the student for several days before implementation to gather baseline levels of behavior. This may help in setting feasible goals for the student.
>
> - *Shift responsibility to the student.* When accurate in rating school performance, have the student write the daily note. This constitutes a shift toward a self-monitoring process.

Selected Resources

Carns, A. W., & Carns, M. R. (1994). Making behavioral contracts successful. *School Counselor, 42*(2), 155–160.

Davies, D. E., & McLaughlin, T. F. (1989). Effects of a daily report card on disruptive behavior in primary students. *Journal of Special Education, 13*(2), 173–181.

Drege, P., & Beare, P. L. (1991). The effect of a token reinforcement system with a time-out backup consequence on the classroom behavior of E/BD students. *Journal of Special Education, 15*(1), 39–46.

Dunlap, L. K. (1991). Using self-monitoring to increase independence. *Exceptional Children, 23*(3), 17–22.

Galloway, J., & Sheridan, S. M. (1994). Implementing scientific practices through case studies: Examples using home-school interventions and consultation. *Journal of School Psychology, 32*(4), 385–413.

Jenson, W. R., Rhode, G., & Reavis, H. K. (1997). *The tough kid tool box.* Longmont, CO: Sopris West.

Levendoski, L. S., & Cartledge, G. (2000). Self-monitoring for elementary school children with serious emotional disturbances: Classroom applications for increased academic responding. *Behavioral Disorders, 25*(3), 211–224.

Olmi, D. J. (1997). Time-in/time-out as a response to noncompliance and inappropriate behavior with children with developmental disabilities: Two case studies. *Psychology in the Schools, 34*(1), 31–39.

Peterson, L. D., Young, K. R., & West, R. P. (1999). Effects of student self-management on generalization of student performance to regular classrooms. *Education and Treatment of Children, 22*(3), 357–372.

Self-Monitoring Planning Guide

Student _____ Date _____

1. Define the behavior that the student will monitor in a way that is easily understood by the child and also observable (e.g., "Staying in my seat and keeping my eyes on my own paper").

   _____

   _____

   _____

2. What will be used to prompt the student to self-monitor (e.g., a signal from the teacher, timer, end of a period or half day)?

   _____

3. How will the student record behavior (e.g., checks, + or - signs, yes/no response)?

   _____

   _____

4. Who will train the student in the procedures to follow when self-monitoring?

   _____

5. When and where will training take place?

   _____

   _____

6. Check off each step of the training as you complete it:

   ❑ Tell the student what behaviors he or she is monitoring.

   ❑ Explain that this is a way to help the student remember which good behaviors he or she is working on and to develop better habits through practice.

   ❑ Teach the student the prompt that will be used.

   ❑ Show the student how to use the recording sheet.

7. How often will random checks be done to check agreement with the student ratings?

   _____

   _____

From *Functional Behavioral Assessment and Intervention in Schools: A Practitioner's Guide (Grades 1–8)*, by J. L. McDougal, S. M. Chafouleas, and B. Waterman, 2006, Champaign, IL: Research Press (800-519-2707; www.researchpress.com)

Daily Self-Monitoring Form 1

Student _____ Date _____

Today this is how well I _____

_____.

During _____

During _____

During _____

During _____

Today I earned _____ smiley faces.

From *Functional Behavioral Assessment and Intervention in Schools: A Practitioner's Guide (Grades 1–8)*, by J. L. McDougal, S. M. Chafouleas, and B. Waterman, 2006, Champaign, IL: Research Press (800-519-2707; www.researchpress.com)

Daily Self-Monitoring Form 2

Student _____ Date _____

Today, this is how well I met the following behavioral expectations:

_____

_____

Morning time 1 _____

❏ Poor   ❏ Fair   ❏ Great

_____

Morning time 2 _____

❏ Poor   ❏ Fair   ❏ Great

_____

Morning time 3 _____

❏ Poor   ❏ Fair   ❏ Great

_____

Number of morning "Greats" _____   Got morning incentive ❏Yes   ❏ No

_____

Afternoon time 1 _____

❏ Poor   ❏ Fair   ❏ Great

_____

Afternoon time 2 _____

❏ Poor   ❏ Fair   ❏ Great

_____

Afternoon time 3 _____

❏ Poor   ❏ Fair   ❏ Great

_____

Number of afternoon "Greats" _____   Got afternoon incentive ❏Yes   ❏ No

_____

From *Functional Behavioral Assessment and Intervention in Schools: A Practitioner's Guide (Grades 1–8),* by J. L. McDougal, S. M. Chafouleas, and B. Waterman, 2006, Champaign, IL: Research Press (800-519-2707; www.researchpress.com)

Daily Self-Monitoring Form 3

Student _____ Date _____

Today, this is how well I met the following expectations:

_____

_____

_____

In the morning				
1	2	3	4	5
Blew It!		Did OK		Did Great!!

In the afternoon				
1	2	3	4	5
Blew It!		Did OK		Did Great!!

Comments _____

_____

_____

_____

From *Functional Behavioral Assessment and Intervention in Schools: A Practitioner's Guide (Grades 1–8)*, by J. L. McDougal, S. M. Chafouleas, and B. Waterman, 2006, Champaign, IL: Research Press (800-519-2707; www.researchpress.com)

Daily Self-Monitoring Form 4

Student _____ Date _____

Behavioral expectations:

_____

_____

This is how I would rate my behavior today:

❏ EXCELLENT

❏ SATISFACTORY

❏ FAIR

❏ POOR

Comments _____

_____

_____

From *Functional Behavioral Assessment and Intervention in Schools: A Practitioner's Guide (Grades 1–8)*, by J. L. McDougal, S. M. Chafouleas, and B. Waterman, 2006, Champaign, IL: Research Press (800-519-2707; www.researchpress.com)

Weekly Self-Monitoring Form 1

Student _____ Date _____

Daily goal _____

Behavioral expectations _____

Circle the number of smiley faces you earned each day.

Monday	Tuesday	Wednesday	Thursday	Friday

From *Functional Behavioral Assessment and Intervention in Schools: A Practitioner's Guide (Grades 1–8)*, by J. L. McDougal, S. M. Chafouleas, and B. Waterman, 2006, Champaign, IL: Research Press (800-519-2707; www.researchpress.com)

WORKSHEET 10.7

Weekly Self-Monitoring Form 2

Student _____ Daily goal _____ Date _____

Behavioral expectations _____

Shade the boxes to show how many "Great" ratings you earned each day.

Monday
6
5
4
3
2
1

Tuesday
6
5
4
3
2
1

Wednesday
6
5
4
3
2
1

Thursday
6
5
4
3
2
1

Friday
6
5
4
3
2
1

From *Functional Behavioral Assessment and Intervention in Schools: A Practitioner's Guide (Grades 1–8)*, by J. L. McDougal, S. M. Chafouleas, and B. Waterman, 2006, Champaign, IL: Research Press (800-519-2707; www.researchpress.com)

WORKSHEET 10.8

Behavior Contract Planning Guide

Student _____ Date _____

1. What behavior(s) is the student expected to perform? (Identify one or two behaviors. Word them positively and clearly, in goal format: behavior, criterion, time frame.)

    a) _____

    b) _____

2. What incentives will be provided for meeting the behavior goal?

    a) _____

    b) _____

    c) _____

3. When will the incentives be delivered? _____

    _____

4. What are the consequences for failure to meet a minimum level of acceptable behavior? *(Optional)*

    _____

    _____

5. How will the student's progress toward the goal be monitored?

    _____

    _____

6. What will the bonus clause for exceptional performance entail? *(Optional)*

    _____

    _____

7. List the dates when the contract will begin and end: _____ to _____

8. Sign the contract (teacher, student, and parents, if appropriate).

From *Functional Behavioral Assessment and Intervention in Schools: A Practitioner's Guide (Grades 1–8)*, by J. L. McDougal, S. M. Chafouleas, and B. Waterman, 2006, Champaign, IL: Research Press (800-519-2707; www.researchpress.com)

Behavior Contract 1

I promise to meet the following expectations:

_____

_____

_____

If I do, my teacher has promised me one of the following rewards:

_____

_____

_____

This is when I get a reward:
This is what I have to do to get a reward:

Bonus for outstanding performance:

_____

Penalty for "just not trying":

_____

Student signature	_Date_	_Teacher signature_	_Date_

Contract dates: _____ to _____

From *Functional Behavioral Assessment and Intervention in Schools: A Practitioner's Guide (Grades 1–8)*, by J. L. McDougal, S. M. Chafouleas, and B. Waterman, 2006, Champaign, IL: Research Press (800-519-2707; www.researchpress.com)

Behavior Contract 2

Expectations

The student, _____, will be expected to do his/her personal best by reaching the following behavioral goals. *(State goals in specific, measurable terms.)*

1. _____

2. _____

Incentives

The student and teacher have agreed to the following incentive options:

1. _____

2. _____

3. _____

4. _____

5. _____

What is required of the student to receive the incentive?

_____

When/how often will the student receive the incentive?

_____

Consequences

List below what will happen if the student does not meet the expectations.

1. _____

2. _____

3. _____

4. _____

Monitoring Plan

How will student progress be monitored?

_____

_____

How often will monitoring occur, and who will conduct it?

_____

_____

From *Functional Behavioral Assessment and Intervention in Schools: A Practitioner's Guide (Grades 1–8)*, by J. L. McDougal, S. M. Chafouleas, and B. Waterman, 2006, Champaign, IL: Research Press (800-519-2707; www.researchpress.com)

(page 1 of 2)

Home or Other Components

List any other intervention components that will be applied with the plan and add any additional notes:

_____

_____

_____

_____

_____

_____

The student's plan will be reviewed in _____ week(s) to assess his/her progress toward identified goals.

We, the undersigned, have read and agree to the plan above.

_____   _____
Teacher signature   *Date*   *Student signature*   *Date*

_____
Parent signature   *Date*

Time-Out Planning Guide

Student _____ Date _____

1. What behaviors will result in time-out (listed in clear, observable terms)?

   _____

   _____

   _____

2. Where will the student be sent for time-out? _____

3. How long will time-out last? _____

4. Will a warning be used prior to time-out? If so, what will it be?

   _____

5. Who will monitor the student during time-out, and where will time-out occur?

   _____

6. What will the student be required to do while in time-out?

   _____

   _____

7. Describe the procedure the student will follow when reentering the classroom.

   _____

   _____

8. Who will explain the time-out procedure to the student and parent?

   _____

9. Describe any multistep time-out plan (e.g., first time-out in room, second in hall, third in office).

   _____

   _____

10. Indicate how the parent will be notified of each time-out episode.

    _____

    _____

From *Functional Behavioral Assessment and Intervention in Schools: A Practitioner's Guide (Grades 1–8)*, by J. L. McDougal, S. M. Chafouleas, and B. Waterman, 2006, Champaign, IL: Research Press (800-519-2707; www.researchpress.com)

Time-Out Supervisor's Guide

Student _____ Date _____

Supervisor _____ Teacher _____

Specific behaviors that will result in time-out:

_____

_____

_____

If minor behaviors can be easily ignored, first try to *ignore the behavior and restate the task.*

For persistent behaviors and the behaviors listed above, quickly and without further interaction, *remove the student to the designated time-out area or room.* This prearranged area should be free from as much stimuli as possible (e.g., include only desk, chair, timer).

Time-out area: _____

The student will remain in the time-out area until the end of the designated time period (e.g., five minutes).

Time-out interval: _____

Once the student is in time-out, there should be no conversation or discussion other than the following prompt:

> You need to demonstrate quiet, calm behavior for _____ (e.g., five) minutes. When you are quiet and sitting, I will start the timer.

If the student talks, yells, or bangs on things, reset the timer and reiterate the prompt.

When the student has completed the designated quiet time, he or she should be quickly returned to class and reintegrated into the lesson, with no extraneous discussion.

From *Functional Behavioral Assessment and Intervention in Schools: A Practitioner's Guide (Grades 1–8),* by J. L. McDougal, S. M. Chafouleas, and B. Waterman, 2006, Champaign, IL: Research Press (800-519-2707; www.researchpress.com)

School-Home Note Planning Guide

Student _____ Date _____

1. What behavior(s) is the student expected to perform? (Behaviors should be clear and positively stated.)

   a) _____

   b) _____

   c) _____

   d) _____

2. Describe the monitoring procedure:

   When will monitoring take place? _____

   Who will carry it out? _____

3. Indicate the student's goal for each behavior:

   a) _____

   b) _____

   c) _____

   d) _____

4. Describe (or attach copies of) any additional intervention components (e.g., incentives, contracts):

   _____

   _____

   _____

From *Functional Behavioral Assessment and Intervention in Schools: A Practitioner's Guide (Grades 1–8)*, by J. L. McDougal, S. M. Chafouleas, and B. Waterman, 2006, Champaign, IL: Research Press (800-519-2707; www.researchpress.com)

School-Home Note

Dear Parent:

This note indicates how positive _____ 's behavior was today in the classroom. A rating of 4 or 5 indicates good progress, 3 suggests fair progress, and 1 or 2 reflects little progress. Please discuss these scores with your child and sign and return the bottom portion of the note to me at school by _____. Thank you.

_____   _____

Teacher signature   *Date*

- -

Student _____ **Date** _____

1. **Completed assigned schoolwork**

1	2	3	4	5
Never	Occasionally	Sometimes	Often	Always

2. **Complied with adult requests without arguing**

1	2	3	4	5
Never	Occasionally	Sometimes	Often	Always

3. **Got along well with other students**

1	2	3	4	5
Never	Occasionally	Sometimes	Often	Always

4. **Other goal:** _____

1	2	3	4	5
Never	Occasionally	Sometimes	Often	Always

5. **Other goal:** _____

1	2	3	4	5
Never	Occasionally	Sometimes	Often	Always

Additional comments:

_____   _____

Parent signature   *Date*

From *Functional Behavioral Assessment and Intervention in Schools: A Practitioner's Guide (Grades 1–8)*, by J. L. McDougal, S. M. Chafouleas, and B. Waterman, 2006, Champaign, IL: Research Press (800-519-2707; www.researchpress.com)

School-Home Progress Monitoring Graph

Student _____ Dates _____ to _____

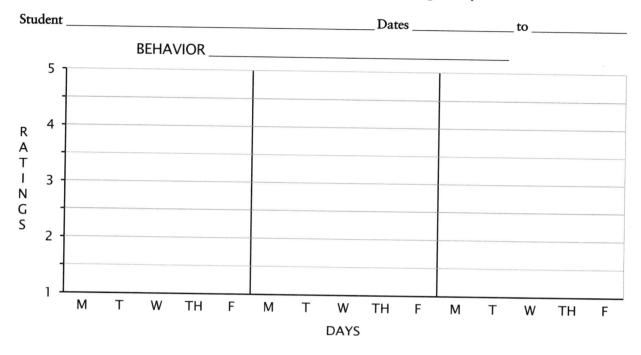

Student _____ Dates _____ to _____

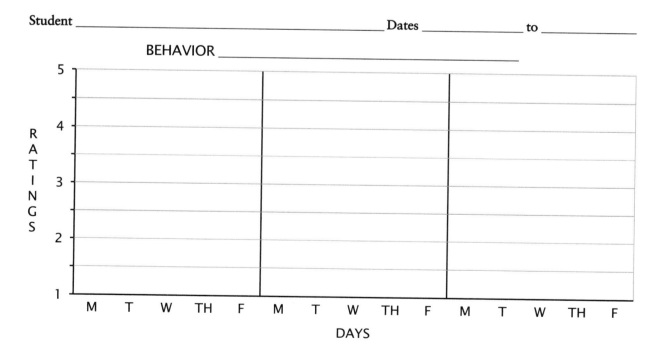

From *Functional Behavioral Assessment and Intervention in Schools: A Practitioner's Guide (Grades 1–8),* by J. L. McDougal, S. M. Chafouleas, and B. Waterman, 2006, Champaign, IL: Research Press (800-519-2707; www.researchpress.com)

CHAPTER 11

Concluding Thoughts

Over the course of the school year, the behavior of 6-year-old Joey has improved. Although he continues to be challenging at times, Joey has been successfully accommodated in his classroom setting. An initial view of Joey's situation might have suggested that school personnel could do little for him because so many of his problems stemmed from out-of-school factors. However, the ongoing problem-solving process of FBA has provided a framework for identifying areas in his life that are changeable, along with a means of matching his needs to meaningful, workable, and sustainable interventions. By providing Joey with additional academic support, altering the teacher's response to his noncompliance, offering him a personal incentive to promote positive behavior, and involving the home in his positive support plan, the educators involved in Joey's case have strengthened his connection to the school environment and increased his ability to adapt to its many demands. Although the FBA process offered no quick fix for the challenges that Joey posed, it has allowed him to continue with his peers and advance academically, socially, and behaviorally.

Functional behavioral assessment (FBA) is a step-by-step process in which specific behavioral problems are clearly defined, antecedents and settings that predict the behavior and the consequences that maintain it are identified, and the functions the behavior serves are recognized. The goal of this process is to aid decision making by providing a match between the assessed problem and the treatment. Interventions usually involve changing the environment, reinforcing positive alternative behaviors, and teaching skills—academic, behavioral, or communicative—the child lacks. Because the level of challenging behavior and thus the need for FBA in the school setting depend somewhat on environmental and instructional variables, the interventions described in this book include a range of skill-based approaches, group and classwide approaches, and individualized plans. Such broad coverage may open us up to criticism because not all the interventions we discuss necessarily require that a comprehensive FBA be performed. As practitioners, we believe that the most economical interventions (in time and resources) that accommodate the student are the best in any given situation. Therefore, as we have already stated, we advocate implementing less intense instructional or group strategies when feasible and reserving the individualized approach for high-intensity behaviors and those high-stakes cases where a more restrictive educational setting may be considered if the challenging behavior persists. The wide range of interventions covered in this book include instructional and group strategies to assist with creating a positive classroom environment in which, if required, individualized FBAs and intervention plans will be more likely to be effective.

Use of the FBA process has been driven by legal, ethical, and practical concerns. Special education law (the Individuals with Disabilities Act and the 1997 amendments to IDEA, or P.L. 105-17) have mandated the use of a process in which behavioral intervention plans are developed and implemented, with direct ties to the FBA process. The 2004 revisions of IDEA (P.L. 108-446) have retained the focus on maintaining students in the least restrictive educational setting, with positive behavioral support. Ethically, it is important to engage in assessment processes that lead to effective, sustainable interventions that can be monitored and revised over time. Finally, the FBA process offers an understandable and feasible means of gathering relevant information on which decisions about a child's education can be based.

The strengths of the FBA process are many and have been reiterated throughout this book. The process leads to the development of hypotheses that can be tested, monitored, evaluated, and revised as needed. It places a child's behavior into a context that makes interventions more meaningful and specific. It emphasizes skills teaching or environmental changes rather than punishment and provides for the encouragement, maintenance, and generalization of new behaviors. Perhaps most important, it emphasizes what can be changed in the educational environment rather than what cannot.

Considerations in the FBA Process

Despite the effectiveness and practicality of the FBA process, a number of questions about it should be answered.

Is FBA Really a New Tool?

Although the use of functional assessment has recently gained momentum, the underlying principles are far from new. The notions that behaviors should be specified and operationalized so that they can be more easily addressed and that behaviors arise from the events that precede or follow them clearly derive from behavioral theory. Application of these principles to the school environment is also not new. Behavior management techniques, behavioral contracts, and token economies have long been used by educators, especially in special education. As Ervin, Ehrhardt, and Poling (2001) have pointed out, however, the early success of interventions based on the principles of operant conditioning was somewhat mediated when those in the field moved away from individualized assessment and treatment to the increased use of punishment or "packaged" interventions. The current FBA process moves back to individualized assessment and intervention design. In essence, functional assessment continues to apply long-standing, scientific principles that encourage careful evaluation of the environmental events that support or diminish behaviors and the institution of interventions that can change or control such behaviors (Ervin, Radford et al., 2001). In addition, contemporary approaches to intervention planning in the schools also emphasize prevention strategies and instructional practices to teach, model, and support prosocial behavior (see Colvin, Sugai, & Patching, 1993; Sugai & Horner, 2002).

When Should FBA Be Used?

Little of the existing research confirms that interventions developed through the FBA process are more effective than those developed in other ways. For example, it is likely that mild or inconsistent problem behaviors may be successfully managed through preventative means (Sugai, Horner, & Sprague, 1999) and may not require the kind of in-depth functional assessment outlined here. The interventions covered in chapters 8 and 9 include some that do not depend on information from a formal FBA. The individualized interventions described in chapter 10 may be informed by an FBA. Furthermore, students who are reacting to definable environmental events, such as the death of a significant person in their life or other trauma, also may not require an FBA to determine effective interventions, which may entail counseling or involvement in support groups. For students who demonstrate behaviors that are seriously and consistently disruptive to their own learning and that of others or who are engaging in dangerous behaviors, however, the use of a more comprehensive FBA may be indicated.

What Does the Research Say?

Although the use of functional assessment has been well researched in individuals who have severe developmental disabilities, it has not been well studied among students who present emotional, academic, or behavioral difficulties but are within the regular education population. The position taken in this book is that functional assessment is a useful process for developing meaningful interventions for a wide range of problems, including behavioral, academic, and communication difficulties; empirically, however, the jury is still out.

A recent review of 100 articles on FBA in school settings suggested that interventions developed as an outcome of the functional assessment process were found to be effective in achieving behavioral change among students with severe disabilities and with those who demonstrated high levels of problem behavior (Ervin et al., 2001b). Despite the positive findings, the authors noted that few of the existing studies examined the effectiveness of FBA among typical students or those with less severe disabilities who were demonstrating behavioral or academic problems in the classroom.

Another recent review identified 22 studies on the use of FBA to inform intervention design for students who possessed emotional or behavioral disorders in school rather than clinical settings (Heckman, Conroy, Fox, & Chait, 2000). The majority of these studies reported positive results. However, sample sizes were small, and most determined the function of a given behavior by descriptive means (i.e., observation, rating scales, interviews) rather than experimental means (i.e., careful manipulation of events in the environment). In addition, although individuals other than the investigators primarily implemented the interventions, less than one-third of the investigators reported the degree to which these individuals actually engaged in the procedures essential to the implementation of the intervention, and few reported long-term maintenance or generalization information (i.e., information on the use of the new behavior in a setting other than where it was taught). Finally, studies that included assessment of social validity suggested that most teachers found the interventions to be relevant and practical to implement. Based on their review, Heckman et al. (2000) have suggested that FBA is a promising procedure, but one that requires additional investigation.

Clearly, we need to know much more about the effectiveness of the FBA process as a tool for instituting and maintaining behavioral change. Current research suggests that, in individual cases, positive change was generally achieved and that the interventions designed were seen as practical and relevant by the teachers who implemented them. Less is known, however, about the maintenance and generalizability of new behaviors generated from functional assessment or the integrity with which teachers or other educators implemented the proposed interventions. Further, it is currently unclear specifically which behaviors warrant an FBA and, if so, what interventions might be most effective for which identified functions. For work with diverse student populations in school settings, more research is needed to answer these important questions.

Is FBA a Valid Process?

To date, very little has been done to establish functional assessment as a valid process. However, validation in the typical sense may be somewhat less critical than with traditional psychological assessment measures because the degree of inference is substantially less with functional assessment. As noted by Shriver, Anderson, and Proctor (2001), the "problem" in traditional assessment is measured as within the child, and thus validity becomes important. In FBA, the problem is viewed as the relationship between the behavior the child manifests and the environment in which it exists. That is, when the behavior a child demonstrates severely interferes with school functioning, an assessment process that can result in positive behavioral change that can be seen and measured is, in a sense, validation in itself.

A framework to provide validation for the FBA process has been proposed by Shriver et al. (2001). As these authors point out, the construct to be validated in functional assessment is the *functional relation*. In FBA, such relations are determined by both direct (observations) and indirect (rating scales or interviews) methods. These authors applied Messick's (1995) six criteria of construct validity to the FBA process. According to Shriver et al., the FBA process should result in (a) the identification of definable, appropriate target and replacement behaviors, (b) the design of meaningful interventions, (c) the sampling of a broad range of environmental antecedents and consequences, (d) an accurate match between the intervention and the setting in which it will be instituted, (e) the identification of relevant cause-effect relationships, and (6) the demonstration of treatment effectiveness. In addition, interrater reliability and generalizability of assessment outcomes across scorers, behaviors, time, settings, method of assessment, dimensions appropriate to the context, and time frame in which the assessment is to be used should be demonstrated. Finally, it is important, according to these authors, that the interventions identified and instituted as an outcome of the FBA process be practical, relevant, and sustainable.

Is the FBA Process Culturally and Personally Sensitive?

Like any tool, functional assessment must be used with skill and sensitivity. As Sheridan (2000) has noted, many of the features of behavioral consultation and functional assessment—such as high level of structure, ecological perspective, objective view of events surrounding a behavior, and emphasis on finding solutions—are inherently more fair and unbiased than other treatment formats. However, these features also highlight the European American values of directness and concrete, linear understanding of problems. Such values are not necessarily cross-cultural. Problems need to be considered in a familial, ethnic, and cultural context. Sheridan cautions that although defining a targeted behavior is an important aspect of functional assessment, some may consider it an impersonalization of the child, thus negatively affecting the relationship between the individuals involved and reducing the likelihood of a positive outcome for the process. She also notes that problems vary among cultures and are influenced by the values of any given family, ethnic, or cultural group:

> The manner in which problems are defined may need to be considered carefully. Brown (1997) noted that some cultural groups attribute more importance to behaviors related to conformity, whereas others value independence and autonomy. For example, defining a problem of a socially withdrawn child as "lacking assertiveness" may be met with resistance. In such cases, a consultant may focus upon specific behaviors and their negative consequences to the child (e.g., "Sam gets teased by his peers and cries a lot as a result") rather than labels ("Sam is passive") or deficiencies ("Sam does not stand up for himself"). (Sheridan, 2000, pp. 346–347)

The goals of the FBA process also need to be considered in ways that make them acceptable and consistent with the values and expectations of the school without ignoring the values of the child or his family or cultural community. Levels of acceptable task completion or accuracy, the prioritizing of the behavior most in need of change, and the timetable in which this change may occur are all factors that may require compromise among the invested parties. Attending to sensitive issues such as (a) a need for personal privacy, (b) the comfort level of the caretaker in making self-disclosures, (c) differences in beliefs about child rearing or academic performance, (d) the availability of resources, (e) skills or other factors that might influence a parent's or caretaker's ability to adhere to an intervention plan, and (f) the levels of trust between the individual or group and school personnel must all be part of the functional assessment process (Sheridan, 2000).

Although virtually no research has examined the use of functional assessment across multicultural contexts, general factors do exist that can be identified to help guide this process. These factors are outlined in Table 11.1.

TABLE 11.1

Guidelines for Sensitive Use of Functional Behavioral Assessment

Guideline	Method of Achieving
Always tend to the "whole child," even when considering interventions for a specific behavior.	Gather information about the child's interests in and out of school, the pressures the child may be under, languages spoken in the home or community, and skills the child possesses.
View the child from within the larger familial and cultural context.	Include interviews and discussions with individuals who know and understand the familial or cultural values and beliefs that may be influencing the antecedents or consequences of a given behavior.
Work for and establish trust among the parties invested in the process.	Establish common goals, identify areas of commonality and differences of belief among the parties involved, listen carefully, recognize and reduce perceived power differences, directly address any racial or cultural concerns.
Keep reports clear and concise.	Limit the use of jargon, use simple and concrete terms, include examples, and clearly describe behaviors and their costs to the child.
Respect privacy.	Don't ask questions that are not directly pertinent to work with the child.
Recognize where the resources are and where they are not.	Take into account parent work demands, the presence of other children, and the availability of funds, transportation, and time for such things as tutoring or involvement in community activities.
Be flexible.	Remember that some problems are culture-specific and that there are usually many possible solutions to a single problem.

Putting It All Together

Clearly, many questions remain about the FBA process. When should it be used? With which students? For what behaviors? Are positive behaviors maintained and generalized to new settings? Is the process valid, culturally sensitive, and acceptable to diverse populations? Although there is much more to learn about the use of these procedures, we believe that FBA and behavioral intervention procedures are valuable tools for accommodating behaviorally challenging students in a variety of school settings. These procedures offer a way to view challenging behavior from a problem-solving standpoint focused on those variables in the environment that are amenable to change. Further, they provide assessment results that are directly tied to intervention and monitoring procedures that involve the use of data in decision making and plan evaluation.

It is our hope that the information and tools presented in this book will be useful to the professionals helping to accommodate students in a variety of applied settings. In our practice, we have found these procedures to be helpful both to the students struggling to adapt to the many demands of their school settings and to the educators working to accommodate them. So, although the empirical evidence on the process continues to come in, we support practitioners in updating and informing their service delivery with such promising practices.

FBA/BIP Worksheets

Functional Behavioral Assessment Worksheet

Student _____ Grade _____ Date _____

Referral source _____ Evaluator _____

Identify and define up to two target behaviors that most interfere with the child's functioning in the classroom. Assess or directly observe the frequency (how often), intensity (high, medium, low), and duration of each.

BEHAVIOR(S)	Frequency	Intensity	Duration

List *distant predictors* identified during interviews/observations (e.g., hunger, lack of sleep, problems on the bus).

_____

_____

_____

_____

Identify any *precursor behaviors* (behaviors exhibited before larger, more intense behavioral episodes), including the reported *behavior chain* (typical sequence of events).

_____

_____

_____

_____

From *Functional Behavioral Assessment and Intervention in Schools: A Practitioner's Guide (Grades 1–8)*, by J. L. McDougal, S. M. Chafouleas, and B. Waterman, 2006, Champaign, IL: Research Press (800-519-2707; www.researchpress.com)

IMMEDIATE ANTECEDENTS AND CONSEQUENCES

From the following list, select the conditions that appear to predict and support each problem behavior. Include the triggers, problematic settings and activities, and consequences.

Triggers/antecedents	Problematic settings/activities	Consequences
❏ Lack of social attention	❏ Independent seatwork	❏ Behavior ignored
❏ Demand/request	❏ Group instruction	❏ Reprimand/warning
❏ Difficult task	❏ Crowded setting	❏ Time-out
❏ Transition (task/setting)	❏ Unstructured activity	❏ Loss of incentives
❏ Specific time of day	❏ Unstructured setting	❏ Sent to office
❏ Interruption in routine	❏ Academic downtime	❏ Home communication
❏ Negative social interaction	❏ Special subjects	❏ In-school suspension
❏ Consequences imposed	❏ Specific task/subject	❏ Out-of-school suspension
❏ Specific people *(List)*	*(List)* _____	❏ Restraint
_____	❏ Other _____	❏ Other _____
_____	❏ Other _____	❏ Other _____

Comments _____

_____

INSTRUCTIONAL AND COMMUNICATIVE NEEDS

Is the student's problem behavior believed to be related to skill deficit or communication needs? *(Check any that apply.)*

Skill deficits		Communication needs
Academic deficit	*Behavioral deficit*	*Communicative intent*
❏ Work is too hard	❏ Lacks the expected behavior	❏ To request assistance
❏ Not enough practice	❏ Needs practice/modeling	❏ To request a break
❏ Not enough help	❏ Requires more structure	❏ To indicate a need
❏ Skill not generalized	❏ Can't apply skill across settings	❏ To indicate frustration
❏ Other _____	❏ Other _____	❏ Other _____

Comments _____

_____

FUNCTIONS OF BEHAVIOR

What function(s) do the identified behavior(s) seem to serve for the child?

To gain something:

Attention/control	**Gain desired item, activity, area**	**Sensory/perceptual feedback**
❏ Gain adult attention	❏ Gain access to a desired item	❏ Gain automatic sensory stimulation
❏ Gain peer attention	❏ Gain access to a desired activity	
❏ Get attention of a preferred adult	❏ Gain access to a desired area	❏ Gain perceptual reinforcement
❏ Other _____	❏ Other _____	❏ Other _____

To escape or avoid something:

❏ Avoid a demand or request   ❏ Avoid a person   ❏ Other _____

❏ Avoid an activity/task (if known)   ❏ Escape the school   ❏ Other _____

Comments _____

_____

FUNCTIONAL THEORY STATEMENT

State hypothesis about behavior in the following form:

When _____ occur(s) in the context of _____,
      (triggers/antecedents)   *(settings/activities)*
the student displays _____ in order to _____,
             (target behavior[s])   *(perceived function)*
and these target behavior(s) may be related to _____.
                                 (skill deficit/communicative intent, when present)

REPLACEMENT BEHAVIORS, PROBLEM-FREE TIMES, AND POTENTIAL MOTIVATORS

Replacement behaviors: What competing adaptive behavior could replace each target behavior and still serve the same function for the student?

_____

_____

When, where, and with whom is the target behavior typically *not* displayed?

_____

_____

List some potential incentives or motivators for the student.

_____

_____

Assessment-to-Intervention Worksheet

Student _____ Grade _____ Date _____

ASSESSMENT INFORMATION

Predictive Conditions	Behaviors	Consequences/Function
Distant:	Desired:	
Precursor behaviors:	Problem:	
Antecedents:	Replacement:	

→

INTERVENTION COMPONENTS

Prevention	Teaching/Support	Alter Consequences
Distant:	Address skill deficits:	New consequences for problem behaviors:
Precursor behaviors:	Teach replacement behaviors:	Reinforcement and monitoring ideas to promote replacement behaviors:
Antecedents:		

From *Functional Behavioral Assessment and Intervention in Schools: A Practitioner's Guide (Grades 1–8)*, by J. L. McDougal, S. M. Chafouleas, and B. Waterman, 2006, Champaign, IL: Research Press (800-519-2707; www.researchpress.com)

Behavior Intervention Plan Worksheet

Student _____ Grade _____ Date _____

Behavioral Goals

State in observable, measurable terms, related to target behaviors.

_____

_____

_____

_____

_____

_____

_____

_____

Detail changes made to prevent the problem (antecedent and setting manipulations):

_____

_____

_____

_____

_____

_____

_____

_____

_____

Indicate teaching and support plan to teach replacement behaviors and address identified skill deficits:

_____

_____

_____

_____

_____

_____

_____

_____

_____

From *Functional Behavioral Assessment and Intervention in Schools: A Practitioner's Guide (Grades 1–8)*, by J. L. McDougal, S. M. Chafouleas, and B. Waterman, 2006, Champaign, IL: Research Press (800-519-2707; www.researchpress.com)

Intervention Steps/Components

Include each step of the intervention, persons responsible, and where and when it will occur. Attach specific intervention forms as applicable. For each intervention:

- Indicate replacement behaviors/roles and how they will be reinforced.

- Identify new consequences imposed for each negative behavior.

- Include a crisis plan for unsafe behavior (if applicable).

_____

_____

_____

_____

_____

_____

_____

_____

_____

_____

Monitoring Student Progress

How will progress be monitored, how often, and by whom?

_____

_____

_____

_____

Monitoring Plan Integrity

How will plan implementation be monitored, how often, and by whom?

_____

_____

_____

_____

Number of instructional weeks before plan will be evaluated _____

Plan review date _____

Plan Evaluation

Indicate student progress toward identified goals.

_____
_____
_____
_____
_____
_____

Indicate the extent to which the intervention was implemented as designed.

_____
_____
_____
_____
_____
_____

How many instructional weeks was the intervention applied? _____

Plan Revisions

Indicate any revisions made to the plan.

_____
_____
_____
_____
_____
_____
_____
_____
_____
_____

Next review date _____

Analyzing Behavior Problems

Analyzing Behavior Problems: Assessment Chart

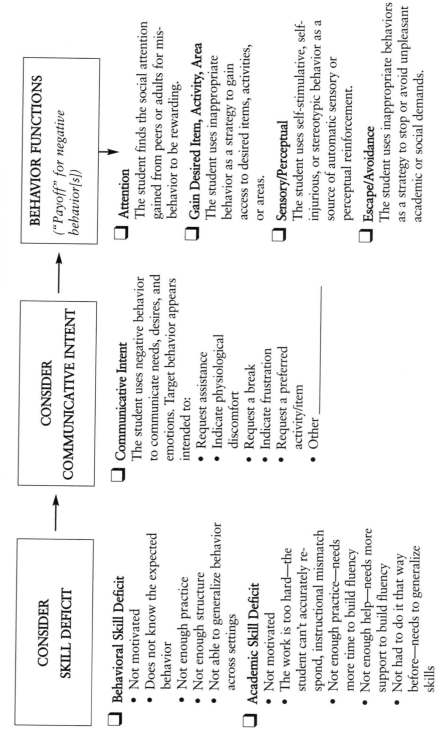

CONSIDER SKILL DEFICIT → **CONSIDER COMMUNICATIVE INTENT** → **BEHAVIOR FUNCTIONS** (*"Payoff" for negative behavior[s]*)

☐ **Behavioral Skill Deficit**
- Not motivated
- Does not know the expected behavior
- Not enough practice
- Not enough structure
- Not able to generalize behavior across settings

☐ **Academic Skill Deficit**
- Not motivated
- The work is too hard—the student can't accurately respond, instructional mismatch
- Not enough practice—needs more time to build fluency
- Not enough help—needs more support to build fluency
- Not had to do it that way before—needs to generalize skills

☐ **Communicative Intent**
The student uses negative behavior to communicate needs, desires, and emotions. Target behavior appears intended to:
- Request assistance
- Indicate physiological discomfort
- Request a break
- Indicate frustration
- Request a preferred activity/item
- Other _____

☐ **Attention**
The student finds the social attention gained from peers or adults for mis-behavior to be rewarding.

☐ **Gain Desired Item, Activity, Area**
The student uses inappropriate behavior as a strategy to gain access to desired items, activities, or areas.

☐ **Sensory/Perceptual**
The student uses self-stimulative, self-injurious, or stereotypic behavior as a source of automatic sensory or perceptual reinforcement.

☐ **Escape/Avoidance**
The student uses inappropriate behaviors as a strategy to stop or avoid unpleasant academic or social demands.

From *Functional Behavioral Assessment and Intervention in Schools: A Practitioner's Guide (Grades 1–8)*, by J. L. McDougal, S. M. Chafouleas, and B. Waterman, 2006, Champaign, IL: Research Press (800-519-2707; www.researchpress.com)

Analyzing Behavior Problems: Intervention Chart

CONSIDER SKILL DEFICIT → **CONSIDER COMMUNICATIVE INTENT** → **BEHAVIOR FUNCTIONS** (*"Payoff" for negative behavior[s]*)

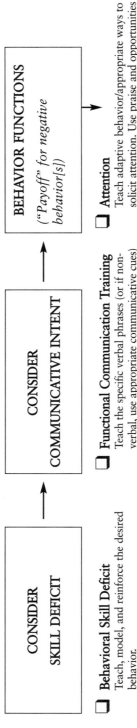

☐ Behavioral Skill Deficit

Teach, model, and reinforce the desired behavior.

- Provide motivator to increase performance
- Teach expected behavior through modeling, practice, and feedback.
- Provide opportunities to practice and receive positive feedback.
- Modify setting to optimize correct performance.
- Provide opportunity for feedback across settings.

☐ Academic Skill Deficit

Use instructional techniques to promote accuracy, fluency, and generalization of skills.

- Provide motivator to increase performance.
- Too hard? Assess student's skills, modify curriculum, ensure instructional match.
- Need more practice? Increase active responding opportunities, use drill and practice techniques and structured teaching tasks.
- Need more assistance? Increase performance feedback. Consider use of response cards, choral tasks, and peer tutors.
- Need to generalize skills? Design applied tasks, promote recognition of when to apply the skill (and when not to), ensure curricular demands to promote skill mastery.

☐ Functional Communication Training

Teach the specific verbal phrases (or if nonverbal, use appropriate communicative cues) to address each of the areas identified in the assessment stage (e.g., solicit adult attention, request assistance, request a break from task).

☐ Steps

- Instruct student in the use of communicative phrase/cues.
- Differentially reinforce (e.g., with praise, attention, task assistance, a break) the functional communication.
- Ensure that negative behavior is no longer reinforced with a functional consequence (see Behavior Functions column).

☐ Attention

Teach adaptive behavior/appropriate ways to solicit attention. Use praise and opportunities for social attention as a reinforcer for adaptive behavior (consider peer tutoring/mentoring, reading to younger students, and enlisting the student in a special role as potential reinforcers). Also ignore or decrease attention for negative behavior (e.g, use time-out).

☐ Gain Desired Item, Activity, Area

Turn desired item, activity, area (or person) into an incentive for positive behavior. Teach adaptive behavior that will result in access to identified reinforcer. Ensure that negative behavior does not result in access to reinforcer.

☐ Sensory/Perceptual

Interrupt automatic reinforcement. Teach alternative/adaptive behavior. Provide incentives offering sensory stimulation (e.g., furry item, Koosh ball, music) as reinforcers to promote positive competing/alternative behaviors.

☐ Escape/Avoidance

Teach cues to solicit assistance with difficult tasks. Increase support for student to persist; reinforce effort. Look for ways to increase the attractiveness of unpleasant demands. Ensure that negative behavior does not result in avoidance of work demands (e.g., student can make up incomplete assignments during free time or after school).

From *Functional Behavioral Assessment and Intervention in Schools: A Practitioner's Guide (Grades 1–8)*, by J. L. McDougal, S. M. Chafouleas, and B. Waterman, 2006, Champaign, IL: Research Press (800-519-2707; www.researchpress.com)

Sample Cases

Elementary Case: Tommy

Middle School Case: Tracy

Functional Behavioral Assessment Worksheet

Student ___Tommy___ Grade ___4___ Date ___3/06/06___

Referral source ___Mrs. Green (classroom teacher)___ Evaluator ___Mr. Sandoval (educational consultant)___

Identify and define up to two target behaviors that most interfere with the child's functioning in the classroom. Assess or directly observe the frequency (how often), intensity (high, medium, low), and duration of each.

BEHAVIOR(S)

BEHAVIOR(S)	Frequency	Intensity	Duration
Class disruptions: Student yells, talks without permission, and makes inappropriate noises (animal imitations) during instructional time.	8–10 times per 45-minute period	low/med	varies

List *distant predictors* identified during interviews/observations (e.g., hunger, lack of sleep, problems on the bus).

None identified at this time.
_____
_____
_____
_____

Identify any *precursor behaviors* (behaviors exhibited before larger, more intense behavioral episodes), including the reported *behavior chain* (typical sequence of events).

Student often begins with smaller disruptions (e.g., quiet talking) and escalates until the teacher redirects him.
_____
_____
_____

From *Functional Behavioral Assessment and Intervention in Schools: A Practitioner's Guide (Grades 1–8),* by J. L. McDougal, S. M. Chafouleas, and B. Waterman, 2006, Champaign, IL: Research Press (800-519-2707; www.researchpress.com)

IMMEDIATE ANTECEDENTS AND CONSEQUENCES

From the following list, select the conditions that appear to predict and support each problem behavior. Include the triggers, problematic settings and activities, and consequences.

Triggers/antecedents	Problematic settings/activities	Consequences
☑ Lack of social attention	☐ Independent seatwork	☑ Behavior ignored
☐ Demand/request	☑ Group instruction	☑ Reprimand/warning
☐ Difficult task	☑ Crowded setting	☑ Time-out
☑ Transition (task/setting)	☑ Unstructured activity	☑ Loss of incentives
☐ Specific time of day	☑ Unstructured setting	☑ Sent to office
☑ Interruption in routine	☐ Academic downtime	☑ Home communication
☐ Negative social interaction	☐ Special subjects	☑ In-school suspension
☐ Consequences imposed	☐ Specific task/subject	☐ Out-of-school suspension
☐ Specific people *(List)*	*(List)* _____	☐ Restraint
_____	☐ Other _____	☐ Other _____
_____	☐ Other _____	☐ Other _____

Comments _____

_____

INSTRUCTIONAL AND COMMUNICATIVE NEEDS

Is the student's problem behavior believed to be related to skill deficit or communication needs? *(Check any that apply.)*

Skill deficits		Communication needs
Academic deficit	*Behavioral deficit*	*Communicative intent*
☐ Work is too hard	☐ Lacks the expected behavior	☐ To request assistance
☐ Not enough practice	☐ Needs practice/modeling	☐ To request a break
☐ Not enough help	☐ Requires more structure	☐ To indicate a need
☐ Skill not generalized	☐ Can't apply skill across settings	☐ To indicate frustration
☐ Other _____	☐ Other _____	☐ Other _____

Comments *None identified at this time.* _____

_____

FUNCTIONS OF BEHAVIOR

What function(s) do the identified behavior(s) seem to serve for the child?

To gain something:

Attention/control	**Gain desired item, activity, area**	**Sensory/perceptual feedback**
☑ Gain adult attention	☐ Gain access to a desired item	☐ Gain automatic sensory stimulation
☑ Gain peer attention	☐ Gain access to a desired activity	
☐ Get attention of a preferred adult	☐ Gain access to a desired area	☐ Gain perceptual reinforcement
☐ Other _____	☐ Other _____	☐ Other _____

To escape or avoid something:

☐ Avoid a demand or request	☐ Avoid a person	☐ Other _____
☐ Avoid an activity/task (if known)	☐ Escape the school	☐ Other _____

Comments _____

FUNCTIONAL THEORY STATEMENT

State hypothesis about behavior in the following form:

When <u>*transitions or lack of teacher attention*</u> occur(s) in the context of <u>*group or unstructured settings*</u>,
　　　　(triggers/antecedents)　　　　　　　　　　　　　　　　　*(settings/activities)*

the student displays _____<u>*disruptive behavior*</u>_____ in order to _____<u>*gain attention*</u>_____,
　　　　　　　　　(target behavior[s])　　　　　　　　　　　　*(perceived function)*

and these target behavior(s) may be related to _____<u>*n/a*</u>_____.
　　　　　　　　　　　　　　　(skill deficit/communicative intent, when present)

REPLACEMENT BEHAVIORS, PROBLEM-FREE TIMES, AND POTENTIAL MOTIVATORS

Replacement behaviors: What competing adaptive behavior could replace each target behavior and still serve the same function for the student?

Hand raising would be a socially appropriate way to elicit teacher attention. Teaching Tommy to tutor younger students could provide an additional opportunity to receive positive social attention.

When, where, and with whom is the target behavior typically *not* displayed?

Tommy is generally well behaved in small groups, during reading group, and with his community mentor.

List some some potential incentives or motivators for the student.

The teacher could encourage hand raising through attention and praise.

Tommy could be provided with peer-tutoring opportunities to reduce his classroom disruptions.

Assessment-to-Intervention Worksheet

ASSESSMENT INFORMATION

Predictive Conditions	Behaviors	Consequences/Function
Distant: *Unknown*	**Desired:** *On-task, raise hand during instruction*	*Positive attention*
Precursor behaviors: *Smaller distractions lead to louder behavior until redirected*	**Problem:** *Class disruption (call-outs, animal noises)*	*Teacher and peer attention*
Antecedents: *Lack of attention, transitions, group instruction*	**Replacement:** *Raise hand instead of calling out, tutor young children*	*Teacher and peer attention*

INTERVENTION COMPONENTS

Prevention	Teaching/Support	Alter Consequences
Distant: *Unknown*	**Address skill deficits:** *None identified.*	**New consequences for problem behaviors:** *Call-outs result in diminished time for peer tutoring. Hand raising is praised and results in attention and peer tutoring time.*
Precursor behaviors: *Develop small visual cue to intervene with low-level disruptions.*	**Teach replacement behaviors:** *Reteach hand raising; model examples; provide frequent praise and attention to "hand raisers."*	**Reinforcement and monitoring ideas to promote replacement behaviors:** *Use peer-tutoring time as incentive to promote hand-raising behavior and reduce call-outs.*
Antecedents: *Cue Tommy for expected behavior before each instructional period. Cue for upcoming transitions. Attend to hand-raising behavior.*	*Teach strategies for tutoring young students; enlist as a tutor in the kindergarten.*	

196

Behavior Intervention Plan Worksheet

Student ___Tommy___ Grade ___4___ Date ___3/06/06___

Behavioral Goals

State in observable, measurable terms, related to target behaviors.

Student will reduce class disruptions to no more than three per instructional period within 3 weeks.

Detail changes made to prevent the problem (antecedent and setting manipulations):

The teacher will:

Use proximity and a visual cue (raised eyebrow) to intervene with low-level disruptive behavior.

Attend to Tommy's hand-raising behavior promptly.

Cue the class prior to transitions (5 min, 1 min, transition time).

Cue the class for the expected behavior (hand raising) and use a game format at least once daily to reinforce the skill.

Indicate teaching and support plan to teach replacement behaviors and address identified skill deficits:

The teacher will:

Discuss the need for hand raising with Tommy and the class.

Have students model both examples and nonexamples of proper hand raising.

The school counselor will:

Show Tommy how to use the self-monitoring form.

Teach Tommy peer-tutoring procedures and enlist him as a tutor for Mrs. Smith's kindergarten class.

Intervention Steps/Components

Include each step of the intervention, persons responsible, and where and when it will occur. Attach specific intervention forms as applicable. For each intervention:

- Indicate replacement behaviors/roles and how they will be reinforced.
- Identify new consequences imposed for each negative behavior.
- Include a crisis plan for unsafe behavior (if applicable).

Before each period of instruction, the teacher will remind Tommy about the expected behavior

   ("Remember, Tommy, during math you need to raise your hand instead of calling out").

Tommy will monitor his class disruptions using a daily self-monitoring form. The teacher will periodi-

   cally check the accuracy of Tommy's ratings throughout the day.

For each academic period in which Tommy meets his goal, he will be allowed to tutor a younger child in

   reading for 5 minutes at the end of the day.

If Tommy's ratings are not consistent with the teacher's (+/–2), then he will not receive this incentive

   for the day.

Each day, the teacher will collect Tommy's monitoring sheet and put it in a folder.

The teacher will inform Tommy's parents of the plan. Each day, the teacher will send a copy of Tommy's

   self-monitoring form home so his parents can review his progress.

Monitoring Student Progress

How will progress be monitored, how often, and by whom?

The teacher will monitor Tommy's progress by collecting his daily self-monitoring sheets and comparing

   them with her own.

Monitoring Plan Integrity

How will plan implementation be monitored, how often, and by whom?

The teacher will check the accuracy of Tommy's monitoring at least once daily.

Number of instructional weeks before plan will be evaluated _____3_____

Plan review date   *3/27/06*

Plan Evaluation

Indicate student progress toward identified goals.

The student has consistently achieved his goal and does enjoy the peer tutoring in Mrs. Smith's room.

Indicate the extent to which the intervention was implemented as designed.

The teacher has collected all daily self-monitoring forms, and the student has self-monitored accurately.

How many instructional weeks was the intervention applied?   *3*

Plan Revisions

Indicate any revisions made to the plan.

Raise student goal to no more than one class disruption per academic period.

In addition to meeting his new behavior goal, Tommy must now also complete his classwork in order to be released for tutoring at the end of the day.

Next review date   *4/17/06*

Functional Behavioral Assessment Worksheet

Student ___*Tracy*_____ Grade ___*8*___ Date ___*2/14/06*_____

Referral source ___*Mr. Burgess (science teacher)*___ Evaluator ___*Ms. Rodgers (school psychologist)*___

Identify and define up to two target behaviors that most interfere with the child's functioning in the classroom. Assess or directly observe the frequency (how often), intensity (high, medium, low), and duration of each.

BEHAVIOR(S)	Frequency	Intensity	Duration
1. Verbal threats toward peers	3–4 times per month	Medium	Short (several seconds)
2. Physical aggression toward peers	1–2 times per month	High	30–60 seconds, or until broken up

List *distant predictors* identified during interviews/observations (e.g., hunger, lack of sleep, problems on the bus).

Earlier peer conflict in the hall or prior classes

_____

_____

_____

Identify any *precursor behaviors* (behaviors exhibited before larger, more intense behavioral episodes), including the reported *behavior chain* (typical sequence of events).

Visible tension/hostility → verbal threats → physical aggression

_____

_____

_____

IMMEDIATE ANTECEDENTS AND CONSEQUENCES

From the following list, select the conditions that appear to predict and support each problem behavior. Include the triggers, problematic settings and activities, and consequences.

Triggers/antecedents	Problematic settings/activities	Consequences
❑ Lack of social attention	❑ Independent seatwork	❑ Behavior ignored
❑ Demand/request	☑ Group instruction	☑ Reprimand/warning
❑ Difficult task	❑ Crowded setting	❑ Time-out
❑ Transition (task/setting)	❑ Unstructured activity	❑ Loss of incentives
❑ Specific time of day	❑ Unstructured setting	☑ Sent to office
❑ Interruption in routine	❑ Academic downtime	☑ Home communication
☑ Negative social interaction	❑ Special subjects	☑ In-school suspension
❑ Consequences imposed	☑ Specific task/subject	❑ Out-of-school suspension
☑ Specific people *(List)*	*(List)* _Science_	❑ Restraint
Sue	❑ Other _____	❑ Other _____
Debbie	❑ Other _____	❑ Other _____

Comments _____

INSTRUCTIONAL AND COMMUNICATIVE NEEDS

Is the student's problem behavior believed to be related to skill deficit or communication needs? *(Check any that apply.)*

Skill deficits		Communication needs
Academic deficit	*Behavioral deficit*	*Communicative intent*
❑ Work is too hard	☑ Lacks the expected behavior	❑ To request assistance
❑ Not enough practice	❑ Needs practice/modeling	❑ To request a break
❑ Not enough help	❑ Requires more structure	❑ To indicate a need
❑ Skill not generalized	❑ Can't apply skill across settings	❑ To indicate frustration
❑ Other _____	❑ Other _____	❑ Other _____

Comments _Tracy's behavior suggests that she does not know how to use nonviolent conflict resolution_
_____ _skills._

FUNCTIONS OF BEHAVIOR

What function(s) do the identified behavior(s) seem to serve for the child?

To gain something:

Attention/control	**Gain desired item, activity, area**	**Sensory/perceptual feedback**
☑ Gain adult attention	❏ Gain access to a desired item	❏ Gain automatic sensory stimulation
☑ Gain peer attention	❏ Gain access to a desired activity	
❏ Get attention of a preferred adult	❏ Gain access to a desired area	❏ Gain perceptual reinforcement
❏ Other _____	❏ Other _____	❏ Other _____

To escape or avoid something:

❏ Avoid a demand or request	❏ Avoid a person	❏ Other _____
❏ Avoid an activity/task (if known)	❏ Escape the school	❏ Other _____

Comments _____

_____

FUNCTIONAL THEORY STATEMENT

State hypothesis about behavior in the following form:

When _____*prior teasing/social conflict*_____ occur(s) in the context of _____*science class/group instruction*_____,
  (triggers/antecedents) *(settings/activities)*
the student displays _*verbal threats/aggression toward peers*_ in order to _____*gain peer and adult attention*_____,
  (target behavior[s]) *(perceived function)*
and these target behavior(s) may be related to _____*a lack of conflict resolution skills*_____.
  (skill deficit/communicative intent, when present)

REPLACEMENT BEHAVIORS, PROBLEM-FREE TIMES, AND POTENTIAL MOTIVATORS

Replacement behaviors: What competing adaptive behavior could replace each target behavior and still serve the same function for the student?

Nonviolent problem-solving approaches—planned ignoring, verbal mediation, requesting a change of work space.

When, where, and with whom is the target behavior typically *not* displayed?

Tracy does not display problem behaviors in other academic classes, where Sue and Debbie are not present.

List some some potential incentives or motivators for the student.

She enjoys social activities with friends, free time, and attention from preferred adults in small groups.

Assessment-to-Intervention Worksheet

Student ___Tracy___   Grade __8__   Date ___2/14/06___

ASSESSMENT INFORMATION

Predictive Conditions	Behaviors	Consequences/Function
Distant: *Earlier peer teasing and/or conflict.*	Desired: *Ignore teasing, walk away from conflict*	*Avoid peer conflict*
Precursor behaviors: *Visible tension and hostility, threatening peers*	Problem: *Threatening peers, physical aggression*	*Peer and adult attention*
Antecedents: *Science class, Sue and Debbie, negative peer interaction (teasing)*	Replacement: *Use problem-solving skills, develop social-helping role with peers*	*Peer and adult attention*

INTERVENTION COMPONENTS

Prevention	Teaching/Support	Alter Consequences
Distant: *Develop check-in procedure at onset of science to report prior peer conflict.*	Address skill deficits: *Enter in social problem solving group, involve Tracy in the school mediation program.*	New consequences for problem behaviors: *Threats will result in assignment to be completed in another classroom. Physical aggression will result in an office referral, phone call home, and short-term suspension of peer mediation duties.*
Precursor behaviors: *Develop alternate work space in the classroom for when Tracy appears tense.*	Teach replacement behaviors: *Teach nonviolent problem solving; planned ignoring, verbal mediation, request a change of seating. Train Tracy as a peer mediator.*	Reinforcement and monitoring ideas to promote replacement behaviors: *Teacher models problem-solving skills. Teacher cues for and praises these skills. Tracy will be trained as peer mediator for other students.*
Antecedents: *Change setting to reduce contact with Sue and Debbie.*		

Behavior Intervention Plan Worksheet

Student ___Tracy_____ Grade __8_____ Date ___2/14/06_____

Behavioral Goals

State in observable, measurable terms, related to target behaviors.

1. Decrease verbal threats towards peers (as observed by science teacher) to 1 or less per week within 4 weeks.

2. Decrease incidents of physical aggression to zero times per month within 4 weeks.

Detail changes made to prevent the problem (antecedent and setting manipulations):

Before science class begins, Tracy will report any prior peer conflict to her science teacher.

The teacher will create an alternative work space for Tracy at the back of the room.

The school psychologist will train Tracy in a check-in procedure with the teacher and show Tracy how to tell the teacher that she needs to use the space.

Indicate teaching and support plan to teach replacement behaviors and address identified skill deficits:

Tracy will complete eight half-hour social problem solving groups with the school psychologist.

She has also expressed interest in becoming a peer mediator, with regular duties 20 minutes per day in the guidance office.

Intervention Steps/Components

Include each step of the intervention, persons responsible, and where and when it will occur. Attach specific intervention forms as applicable. For each intervention:

• Indicate replacement behaviors/roles and how they will be reinforced.

• Identify new consequences imposed for each negative behavior.

• Include a crisis plan for unsafe behavior (if applicable).

The science teacher will model problem-solving skills, as described by the school psychologist, at least once per day. The teacher will also provide cues for these skills when relevant social situations arise and praise Tracy for using these skills.

The peer mediation coordinator will train Tracy as a peer mediator and arrange for 20 minutes of release time per day to perform those duties in the guidance office.

New consequences: Verbal threats will result in an assignment to be completed in another classroom and suspension of peer mediation duties for the day. Physical aggression will result in an office referral, phone call home, and suspension of peer mediation duties for 1 week.

Tracy will complete a behavior contract listing her goals, behavioral expectations, and consequences for problem behavior. Tracy, Tracy's mom, and the science teacher, school psychologist, and school administrator will sign it.

Home component: Each Friday, the school psychologist will send home a report on Tracy's progress in school and involvement in the peer mediation program.

Monitoring Student Progress

How will progress be monitored, how often, and by whom?

The science teacher will record instances of verbal threats and physical aggression via the behavior-log technique.

The school psychologist will monitor Tracy's progress in problem-solving group and involvement in peer mediation weekly, using a modified version of the DBRC.

Monitoring Plan Integrity

How will plan implementation be monitored, how often, and by whom?

The science teacher will document his daily cueing, modeling, and praising of problem-solving skills.

The school psychologist will keep attendance for problem-solving group and peer mediation.

Permanent products (monitoring forms) will be kept on file.

Number of instructional weeks before plan will be evaluated _____4_____

Plan review date ___3/14/06___

Plan Evaluation

Indicate student progress toward identified goals.

Tracy has had no incidents of physical aggression in the last 4 weeks but was observed to threaten Debbie twice.

She has earned positive weekly ratings from the school psychologist for participating in group and peer mediation.

Tracy missed two days of peer mediation for verbal threats.

Indicate the extent to which the intervention was implemented as designed.

Tracy's science teacher rates intervention integrity as high, although he indicates that lately he has not been modeling problem-solving skills unless a conflict situation arises in the classroom.

How many instructional weeks was the intervention applied? ___4___

Plan Revisions

Indicate any revisions made to the plan.

The school psychologist will reinstruct Tracy in verbal mediation skills and alternatives to threatening others.

The science teacher will present at least one weekly problem-solving skill to the class and model, cue, and socially reinforce that skill.

The goal for verbal threats will be reduced to zero instances per week.

Next review date ___4/14/06___

References

Alarćon, M., DeFries, J. C., Ligh, J. G., & Pennington, B. F. (1997). A twin study of mathematics disabilities. *Journal of Learning Disabilities, 30,* 617–623.

Alber, S. R., & Heward, W. L. (1997). Recruit it or lose it! Training students to recruit positive teacher attention. *Intervention in School and Clinic, 32*(5), 275–282.

Alessi, G. J. (1988). Direct observation methods for emotional/behavior problems. In E. S. Shapiro & T. R. Kratochwill (Eds.), *Behavioral assessment in schools: Conceptual foundations and practical applications* (pp. 14–75). New York: Guilford Press.

Atkinson, D. R., & Lowe, S. M. (1995). The role of ethnicity, culture, knowledge, and conventional techniques in counseling and psychotherapy. In J. G. Ponterotto, J. M. Casas, L. A. Sazuki, & C. M. Alexander (Eds.), *Handbook of multicultural counseling* (pp. 387–414). Newbury Park, CA: Sage.

Bauer, A. M., Keefe, C. H., & Shea, T. M. (2001). *Students with learning disabilities or emotional/behavioral disorders.* Upper Saddle River, NJ: Merrill/Prentice Hall.

Bergan, J. R., & Tombari, M. L. (1975). The analysis of verbal interactions occurring during consultation. *Journal of School Psychology, 13,* 209–226.

Bergan, J. R., & Tombari, M. L. (1976). Consultant skill and efficiency and the implementation and outcomes of consultation. *Journal of School Psychology, 14,* 3–14.

Berkowitz, M. J., & Martens, B. K. (2001). Assessing teachers' and students' preferences for school-based reinforcers: Agreement across methods and different effort requirements. *Journal of Developmental and Physical Disabilities, 13,* 373–387.

Biglan, A. (1995). Translating what we know about the context of antisocial behavior into a lower prevalence of such behavior. *Journal of Applied Behavior Analysis, 28,* 479–492.

Blachman, B.A., Ball, E. W., Black, R. S., & Tangel, D. M. (2000). *Road to the code: A phonological awareness program for young children.* Baltimore: Brookes Publishing Company.

Blair, T. R. (1984). Teacher effectiveness: The know-how to improve student learning. *Reading Teacher, 38,* 138–142.

Braaten, S. (1998). *BOS: Behavioral Objective Sequence* (Assessment Manual and Software Program). Champaign, IL: Research Press.

Braden, J. P., & Kratochwill, T. R. (1997). Treatment utility of assessment: Myths and realities. *School Psychology Review, 26,* 475–485.

Bronfenbrenner, U. (1970). *Two worlds of childhood.* New York: Russell Sage Foundation.

Brown, D. (1997). Implications of cultural values for cross-cultural consultation with families. *Journal of Counseling and Development, 76,* 29–35.

Bruning, R. H., Schraw, G. J., & Ronning, R. R. (1999). *Cognitive psychology and instruction.* Upper Saddle River, NJ: Merrill.

Carr, E. G. (1977). The motivation of self-injurious behavior: A review of some hypotheses. *Psychological Bulletin, 84,* 800–816.

Carroll, J. B. (1963). A model of school learning. *Teachers College Record, 64,* 723–733.

Chafouleas, S. M., Riley-Tillman, T. C., & McDougal, J. (2002). Good, bad, or in between: How does the daily behavior report card rate? *Psychology in the Schools, 39,* 157–169.

Cherkes-Julkowski, M. (1998). Learning disability, attention deficit disorder, and language impairment as outcome of prematurity: A longitudinal descriptive study. *Journal of Learning Disabilities, 31,* 194–306.

Christenson, S. L., & Buerkle, K. (1999). Families as educational partners for children's school success: Suggestions for school psychologists. In C. Reynolds & T. Gutkin (Eds.), *Handbook of school psychology* (3rd ed.; pp. 709–744). New York: Wiley.

Christenson, S. L., Rounds, T., & Gorney, D. (1992). Family factors and student achievement: An avenue to increase students' success. *School Psychology Quarterly, 7,* 178–206.

Christenson, S. L., Ysseldyke, J. E., & Thurlow, M. L. (1989). Critical instructional factors for students with mild handicaps: An integrative review. *Remedial and Special Education, 10,* 21–31.

Colvin, G., Sugai, G., & Patching, W. (1993). Pre-correction: An instructional strategy for managing predictable behavior problems. *Intervention, 28,* 143–150.

Cone, J. D. (1978). The behavioral assessment grid (BAG): A conceptual framework and a taxonomy. *Behavior Therapy, 9,* 882–888.

Copps, S. C. (1992). *The attending physician: Attention deficit disorder.* Atlanta: SPI Press.

Crabbe, J. D., McSwigan, J. D., & Kelknap, J. K. (1985). The role of genetics in substance abuse. In M. Galizio & S. A. Maisto (Eds.), *Determinants of substance abuse* (pp. 13–54). New York: Plenum.

Crittenden, P. M. (1989). Teaching maltreated children in the preschool. *Topics in Early Childhood Special Education, 2,* 25–73.

Crone, D. A., & Horner, R. H. (2000). Contextual, conceptual, and empirical foundations of functional behavioral assessment methods in schools. *Exceptionality, 8,* 161–172.

Daly, E. J. III, Lentz, F. E., & Boyer, J. (1996). The instructional hierarchy: A conceptual model for understanding the effective components of reading interventions. *School Psychology Quarterly, 11,* 369–386.

Daly, E. J. III, Witt, J. C., Martens, B. K., & Dool, E. J. (1997). A model for conducting a functional analysis of academic performance problems. *School Psychology Review, 26,* 554–574.

Dauber, S. L., & Epstein, J. L. (1993). Parents' attitudes and practices of involvement in inner city elementary and middle schools. In N. Chavkin (Ed.), *Families and schools in a pluralistic society* (pp. 53–72). Albany: State University of New York Press.

Demchak, M. A. (1993). Functional assessment of problem behaviors in applied settings. *Intervention in School and Clinic, 29,* 89–95.

Drasgow, E., & Yell, M. L. (2001). Functional behavioral assessments: Legal requirements and challenges. *School Psychology Review, 30,* 239–251.

Dyer, K., Dunlap, G., & Winterling, V. (1990). The effects of choice-making on the serious problem behaviors of students with developmental disabilities. *Journal of Applied Behavioral Analysis, 23,* 515–524.

Epstein, J. L. (1995, May). School/family/community partnerships: Caring for the children we share. *Phi Delta Kappan,* pp. 701–712.

Erchul, W. P., & Martens, B. K. (2002). *School consultation: Conceptual and empirical bases of practice* (2nd ed.). New York: Plenum Press.

Ervin, R. A., Ehrhardt, K. E., & Poling, A. (2001a). Functional assessment: Old wine in new bottles. *School Psychology Review, 30,* 173–179.

Ervin, R. A., Radford, P. M., Bertsch, K., Piper, A. L., Ehrhardt, K. E., & Poling, A. (2001b). A descriptive analysis and critique of the empirical literature on school-based functional assessment. *School Psychology Review, 30,* 193–210.

Gambrell, L. B., Pfeiffer, W. R., & Wilson, R. M. (1985). The effects of retelling upon reading comprehension and recall of text information. *Journal of Educational Research, 78,* 216–220.

Gettinger, M., & Stoiber, K. C. (1999). Excellence in teaching: Review of instructional and environmental variables. In C. Reynolds & T. Gutkin (Eds.), *Handbook of school psychology* (3rd ed.; pp. 933–958). New York: Wiley.

Goldstein, A. P., & McGinnis, E. (1997). *Skillstreaming the adolescent: New strategies and perspectives for teaching prosocial skills.* Champaign, IL: Research Press.

Good, T. L., & Brophy, J. E. (1984). *Looking in classrooms* (3rd ed.). New York: Harper & Row.

Gravois, T. A., & Gickling, E. E. (2002). Best practices in curriculum-based assessment. In A. Thomas & J. Grimes (Eds.), *Best practices in school psychology* (pp. 885–898). Bethesda, MD: National Association of School Psychologists.

Green, R. (1992). Learning to learn and the family system: New perspectives on underachievement and learning disorders. In M. J. Fine & C. Carlson (Eds.), *Handbook of family-school interventions: A systems perspective* (pp. 157–174). Boston: Allyn & Bacon.

Greenwood, C. R., & Carta, J. J. (1994). *Ecobehavioral Assessment Systems Software.* Kansas City: Juniper Gardens Children's Center.

Gresham, F. M., Watson, T. S., & Skinner, C. H. (2001). Functional behavioral assessment: Principles, procedures, and future directions. *School Psychology Review, 30,* 156–172.

Handwerk, M. L., & Marshall, R. M. (1998). Behavioral and emotional problems of students with learning disabilities, serious emotional disturbance, or both conditions. *Journal of Learning Disabilities, 31*(4), 327–339.

Haring, N. G., Lovitt, T. C., Eaton, M. D., & Hansen, C. L. (1978). *The fourth R: Research in the classroom.* Columbus, OH: Merrill.

Heckman, K., Conroy, M., Fox, J., & Chait, A. (2000). Functional assessment-based intervention research on students with or at risk for emotional and behavioral disorders in school settings. *Behavioral Disorders, 25,* 196–210.

Holland, E. L., & McLaughlin, T. F. (1982). Using public posting and group consequences to manage student behavior during supervision. *Journal of Educational Research, 76,* 1, 29–34.

Horner, R. H., Diemer, S. M., & Brazeau, K. C. (1992). Educational support for students with severe problem behaviors in Oregon: A descriptive analysis from the 1987–1988 school year. *Journal of the Association of Persons with Severe Handicaps, 17,* 154–169.

Ingraham, C. L. (2000). Consultation through a multicultural lens: Multicultural and cross-cultural consultation in schools. *School Psychology Review, 29,* 321–334.

Iwata, B., Dorsey, M., Slifer, K., Bauman, K., & Richman, G. (1982). Toward a functional analysis of self-injury. *Analysis and Intervention in Developmental Disabilities, 2,* 3–20.

Jenson, W. R., Rhode, G., & Reavis, H. K. (1994). *The tough kid tool box.* Longmont, CO: Sopris West.

Jones, D. B., & Van Houton, R. S. (1985). The use of daily quizzes and public posting to decrease the disruptive behavior of secondary school students. *Education and Treatment of Children, 8*(2), 91–106.

Kauffman, J. (1997). *Characteristics of emotional and behavior disorders of children and youth* (6th ed.). Columbus, OH: Merrill.

Knoff (2002). *The Stop and Think Social Skills Training Program.* Longmont, CO: Sopris West.

Lambert, N. M. (1976). Children's problems and classroom interventions from the perspective of classroom teachers. *Professional Psychology, 7,* 507–517.

Lewis, T. J., & Sugai, G. (1999). Effective behavior support: A systems approach to proactive schoolwide management. *Focus on Exceptional Children, 31,* 1–24.

Mace, F. C., Lalli, J. S., & Lalli, E. P. (1991). Functional assessment and treatment of aberrant behavior. *Research in Developmental Disabilities, 12,* 155–180.

Martens, B. K., Witt, J. C., Daly, E. J., & Vollmer, T. R. (1999). Behavior analysis: Theory and practice in educational settings. In C. Reynolds & T. Gutkin (Eds.), *Handbook of school psychology* (3rd ed.; pp. 638–663). New York: Wiley.

McDougal, J. L. (1998). Disciplining students with disabilities based on the reauthorization of IDEA: An educator's guide to functional behavioral assessment and intervention planning. *NASP Communique, 26*(8).

McDougal, J. L. (1999). Effective classroom based intervention for young aggressive youth. *NASP Communique, 28*(1).

McDougal, J. L., & Chafouleas, S. M. (2001). Behavioral and functional assessment. In J. F. Carlson & B. B. Waterman (Eds.), *Social and personal assessment of school-aged children: Developing interventions for educational and clinical settings.* Needham Heights, MA: Allyn and Bacon.

McDougal, J. L., Clark, K. C., & Wilson, J. (2005). Graphing made easy: Practical tools for school psychologists. *NASP Communique, 34,* Insert 1–6.

McDougal, J. L., & Clonan, S. (2002). Positive behavioral support services: Principles of organizational change and the Syracuse experience. *NASP Communique, 30*(6).

McDougal, J. L., & Clonan, S., & Martens, B. K. (2002). Using organizational change procedures to promote the acceptability of prereferral intervention services: The School-Based Intervention Team project. *School Psychology Quarterly, 15,* 149–171.

McDougal, J. L., Nastasi, B., & Chafouleas, S. M. (2005). Bringing research into practice to intervene with young behaviorally challenging students in public school settings: Evaluation of the Behavior Consultation Team (BCT) project. *Psychology in the Schools, 42,* 537–551.

McGinnis, E., & Goldstein, A. P. (1997). *Skillstreaming the elementary school child: New strategies and perspectives for teaching prosocial skills.* Champaign, IL: Research Press.

McLoyd, V. C. (1998). Socioeconomic disadvantage and child development. *American Psychologist, 53*(2), 185–204.

Mercer, C. D., & Mercer, A. R. (1998). *Teaching students with learning problems* (5th ed.). Upper Saddle River, NJ: Merrill/Prentice-Hall.

Messick, S. (1995). Validity of psychological assessment: Validation of inferences from persons' responses and performance as scientific inquiry into score meaning. *American Psychologist, 50,* 741–749.

Meyer, L. H., & Evans, I. M. (1989). *Nonaversive intervention for behavior problems: A manual for home and community.* Baltimore: Paul H. Brookes.

Moore, L. A., Waguespack, A. M., Wickstrom, K. F., Witte, J. C., & Gaydos, G. R. (1994). Mystery motivator: An effective and time-efficient intervention. *School Psychology Review, 23,* 106–118.

Motram, L., Bray, M. A., Kehle, T. J., Broudy, M., & Jenson, W. R. (in press). Effect of mystery motivators on decreasing disruptive classroom behaviors. *Journal of Applied School Psychology.*

Mullen, P. E., Martin, J. L., Anderson, J. C., Romans, S. E., & Herbison, G. P. (1996). The long-term impact of the physical, emotional, and sexual abuse of children: A community study. *Child Abuse and Neglect, 20*(1), 7–21.

New York State Education Department (1998, July). *Guidance on functional assessments for students with disabilities.* Albany: University of the State of New York.

Noell, G. H., VanDerHeyden, A. M., Gatti, S. L., & Whitmarsh, E. L. (2001). Functional assessment of the effects of escape and attention on students' compliance during instruction. *School Psychology Quarterly, 16,* 253–269.

O'Neill, R. E., Horner, R. H., Albin, R. W., Sprague, J. R., Storey, K., & Newton, J. S. (1997). *Functional assessment and program development for problem behavior: A practical handbook* (2nd ed.). Pacific Grove, CA: Brooks/Cole.

Pajares, F. (1996). Self-efficacy beliefs in academic settings. *Review of Educational Research, 66,* 543–578.

Paul, S. M. (1980). Sibling resemblance in mental ability: A review. *Behavior Genetics, 10,* 277–290.

Prater, L. P. (1992). Early pregnancy and academic achievement of African-American youth. *Exceptional Children, 59,* 141–149.

Quinn, K., & McDougal, J. L. (1998). A mile wide and a mile deep: Comprehensive interventions for children and youth with emotional and behavioral disorders and their families. *School Psychology Review, 27,* 191–203.

Ramey, C. T., & Ramey, S. L. (1998). Early intervention and early experience. *American Psychologist, 53*(2), 109–120.

Ramirez, S. Z., Lepage, K. M., Kratochwill, T. R., & Duffy, J. L. (1998). Multicultural issues in school-based consultation: Conceptual and research considerations. *Journal of School Psychology, 36,* 479–509.

Reid, R., & Nelson, J. R. (2002). The utility, acceptability, and practicality of functional behavioral assessment for students with high-incidence problem behaviors. *Remedial and Special Education, 23,* 15–23.

Repp, A. (1994). Comments on functional analysis procedures for school-based behavior problems. *Journal of Applied Behavior Analysis, 27,* 409–411.

Rhode, G., Jenson, W. R., & Reavis, H. K. (1992). *The tough kid book* (2nd ed.). Longmont, CO: Sopris West.

Rock, E. E., Fessler, M. A., & Church, R. P. (1997). The concomitance of learning disabilities and emotional/behavioral disorders: A conceptual model. *Journal of Learning Disabilities, 30,* 242–244.

Rosenberg, M. S. (1997). Learning disabilities occurring concomitantly with other disability and exceptional conditions: Introduction to the Special Series. *Journal of Learning Disabilities, 30,* 242–244.

Saudargas, R. A. (1997). *State-Event Classroom Observation System (SECOS).* Knoxville: Department of Psychology, University of Tennessee.

Saudargas, R. A., & Lentz, F. E. (1986). Estimating percent of time and rate via direct observation: A suggested observational procedure and format. *School Psychology Review, 15,* 36–48.

Schilling, D., & Cuvo, A. J. (1983). The effects of a contingency-based lottery on the behavior of a special education class. *Education and Training of the Mentally Retarded, 18*(1), 52–58.

Shapiro, E. S. (1996a). *Academic skills problems: Direct assessment and intervention* (2nd ed.). New York: Guilford Press.

Shapiro, E. S. (1996b). *Academic skills problems workbook.* New York: Guilford Press.

Sheridan, S. M. (2000). Considerations of multiculturalism and diversity in behavioral consultation with parents and teachers. *School Psychology Review, 29,* 344–353.

Shriver, M. D., Anderson, C. M., & Proctor, B. (2001). Evaluating the validity of functional behavior assessment. *School Psychology Review, 30,* 180–192.

Smith, J. O. (1995). Behavior management: Getting to the bottom of social skills deficits. *LD Forum, 21*(1), 23–26.

Sprick, R. S. (1985). *Discipline in the secondary classroom: A problem-by-problem survival guide.* West Nyack, NY: Center for Applied Research in Education.

Sprague, J., Sugai, G., & Walker, H. (1998). Antisocial behavior in schools. In T. S. Watson & F. M. Gresham (Eds.), *Handbook of child behavior therapy* (pp. 451–474). New York: Plenum Press.

Sugai, G., & Horner, R. (2002). Introduction to the special series on positive behavior support in the schools. *Journal of Emotional and Behavioral Disorders, 10,* 129–192.

Sugai, G., Horner, R., & Sprague, J. (1999). Functional assessment-based behavior support planning: Research to practice to research. *Behavioral Disorders, 24,* 253–257.

Sugai, G., Sprague, J. R., Horner, R. H., & Walker, H. M. (2000). Preventing school violence: The use of office discipline referrals to assess and monitor school-wide discipline interventions. *Journal of Emotional and Behavioral Disorders, 8,* 94–101.

Sulzer-Azaroff, B., & Mayer, G. R. (1991). *Behavior analysis for lasting change.* Chicago: Holt, Rinehart, and Winston.

Telzrow, C. F., & Beebe, J. J. (2002). Best practices in facilitating intervention adherence and integrity. In A. Thomas & J. Grimes (Eds.), *Best practices in school psychology* (4th ed.; pp. 483–501). Bethesda, MD: National Association of School Psychologists.

Theodore, L. A., Bray, M. A., Kehle, T. J., & Jenson, W. R. (2000). The use of group dependent and randomization procedures to reduce disruptive classroom behavior. *Journal of School Psychology, 39,* 267–277.

Tilly, W. D. III, & Flugum, K. R. (1995). Best practices in ensuring quality interventions. In A. Thomas & J. Grimes (Eds.), *Best practices in school psychology* (3rd ed.; pp. 485–500). Bethesda, MD: National Association of School Psychologists.

Todd, A. W., Horner, R. H., Sugai, G., & Colvin, G. (1999). Individualizing schoolwide discipline for students with chronic problem behaviors: A team approach. *Effective School Practices, 17,* 72–82.

Topping, K. (1987). Paired reading: A powerful technique for parent use. *Reading Teacher, 40,* 608–614.

Tur-Kaspa, H., Wesel, A., & Segev, L. (1998). Attributions for feelings of loneliness of students with learning disabilities. *Learning Disabilities Research and Practice, 13*(2), 160–171.

Upah, K. R., & Tilly, W. D. III. (2002). Best practices in designing, implementing, and evaluating quality interventions. In A. Thomas & J. Grimes (Eds.), *Best practices in school psychology* (4th ed.; pp. 483–501).Bethesda, MD: National Association of School Psychologists.

Vollmer, T. R., & Northrup, J. (1996). Some implications of functional analysis for school psychologists. *School Psychology Quarterly, 11,* 76–92.

Walker, H. M., Colvin, G., & Ramsey, E. (1995). *Antisocial behavior in school: Strategies and best practices.* Pacific Grove, CA: Brooks/Cole.

Waterman, B. (2002). Information-processing perspectives in understanding social and personal behavior. In J. F. Carlson & B. B. Waterman (Eds.), *Social and personality assessment of school-aged children: Developing interventions for educational and clinical use* (pp. 142–157). Boston: Allyn & Bacon.

Weeks, M., & Gaylord-Ross, R. (1981). Task difficulty and aberrant behavior in severely handicapped students. *Journal of Applied Behavior Analysis, 14,* 449–463.

West, R. P., & Sloane, H. N. (1986). Teacher presentation rate and point delivery rate. *Behavior Modification, 10,* 267–286.

Witt, J. C., Daly, E. M., & Noell, G. (2000). *Functional assessments: A step-by-step guide to solving academic and behavior problems.* Longmont, CO: Sopris West.

Witt, J. C., & Elliott, S. N. (1982). The response-cost lottery: A time efficient and effective classroom intervention. *Journal of School Psychology, 20*(2), 155–161.

Wolery, M., Bailey, D. B., & Sugai, G. M. (1988). *Effective teaching: Principles and procedures of applied behavior analysis with exceptional students.* Needham, MA: Allyn & Bacon.

Wolf, M. M. (1978). Social validity: The case for subjective measurement, or how applied behavior analysis is finding its heart. *Journal of Applied Behavior Analysis, 11,* 203–214.

Ysseldyke, J. E., & Christenson, S. L. (1993). *The Instructional Environment System-II.* Longmont, CO: Sopris West.

Ysseldyke, J. E., & Elliott, J. (1999). Effective instructional practices: Implications for assessing educational environments. In C. Reynolds & T. Gutkin (Eds.), *Handbook of school psychology* (3rd ed.; pp. 497–518). New York: Wiley.

About the Authors

JAMES L. MCDOUGAL, PSY.D., is an assistant professor in the school psychology program in the Counseling and Psychological Services Department at The State University of New York at Oswego. He was formerly the mental health coordinator for the Syracuse City School District, where he provided mental health and behavioral consultation services to over 40 schools and programs. Dr. McDougal has 15 years of experience as a practicing school psychologist and has consulted on issues relating to students with academic and behavioral problems. He has presented numerous training seminars at state and national forums in the areas of school-based functional assessment, academic and behavioral intervention planning, consultation, and prereferral intervention. Dr. McDougal also has a considerable record of scholarly publication.

SANDRA M. CHAFOULEAS, PH.D., is currently an associate professor in the Neag School of Education at the University of Connecticut. Dr. Chafouleas received her Ph.D. from Syracuse University and is a licensed psychologist in Connecticut. She has taught courses in behavior assessment and intervention, academic and intellectual assessment, ethics, and the roles and functions of school psychologists. Dr. Chafouleas is currently serving as an associate editor for *School Psychology Review* and as guest editor and board member for *Psychology in the Schools*. Her primary areas of research involve the prevention of reading difficulties and the application of evidence-based strategies to the classroom. She has authored or coauthored over 30 refereed journal articles, book chapters, and books. Prior to becoming a university trainer, Dr. Chafouleas worked as a school psychologist and school administrator in a variety of settings dealing with children with behavior disorders.

BETSY WATERMAN, PH.D., is a professor and chair of the Counseling and Psychological Services Department at The State University of New York at Oswego, where she teaches in a graduate program that trains school psychologists and counselors. She is also an active researcher in the area of learning problems, reading, memory, and early childhood. A licensed psychologist with a background in special education, she taught students with emotional disabilities prior to her work as a school psychologist and college professor. Dr. Waterman also worked as part of a preschool assessment team for several years and currently is a mental health consultant to Head Start in Oswego County. She is a regular presenter on a variety of topics internationally, nationally, and regionally.